How to

DRINK
LIKE A
ROCK STAR

Recipes for the Cocktails and Libations
that Inspired 100 Music Legends

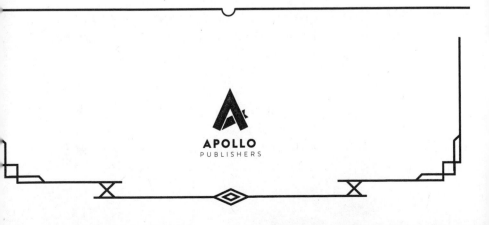

APOLLO
PUBLISHERS

How to Drink Like a Rock Star: Recipes for the Cocktails
and Libations that Inspired 100 Music Legends
Copyright © 2022 by Apollo Publishers

Visit our website at www.apollopublishers.com.

Published in compliance with California's Proposition 65.

Library of Congress Control Number: 2022935462

Writing by Julia Abramoff.
Interior illustrations by Catherine A. Moore.
Cover and interior design by Rain Saukas.

Front cover photos left to right: 1. Lenny Kravitz, WENN Rights Ltd /Alamy Stock Photo; 2. Mick Jagger, Keystone Press / Alamy Stock Photo; 3. Joni Mitchell, Barry King / Alamy Stock Photo; 4. Gwen Stefani, The Photo Access / Alamy Stock Photo.

Print ISBN: 978-1-954641-06-8
Ebook ISBN: 978-1-954641-07-5

Printed in the United States of America.

CONTENTS

INTRODUCTION

"I never drink anything before a show; afterwards, just a glass of wine to make the return journey to the real world a little less traumatic." —Suzi Quatro

On the pages that follow we've selected one hundred of rock's greatest musicians and bands and present with them the stars' drinks of choice to court the music muse. This is but a sampling of some of the defining voices of rock history and is in no way a definitive list. And while all featured legends are certainly "rock stars," a great many have embraced a fusion of musical styles.

To determine each star's drink of choice, we have made best efforts for authenticity, with a deep dive into the stars' memoirs and interviews, their backstage tour riders, photos of them, biographies of them, documentaries about them, even their social media feeds and their lyrics. We recognize that rock and roll has historically had deep ties to drug and alcohol abuse, and efforts have been made to recognize those who've fallen and those who've overcome. To this end, we often offer mocktail substitution suggestions out of respect and so everyone can enjoy, and always provide recommended serving sizes. One drink to channel a legend should be sufficient when their tunes are playing on high.

In addition to recipes, you'll find occasional notes on favorite food pairings and hangover cures, a guide to the bar tools to stock up on and the libations to have on hand, as well as profiles of the stars, quotes, and a section on epic rock clubs to drink, dance, and perform in. Now turn up the music, gather your bar tools, and let's get to it.

BAR TOOLS

Cocktail shaker

Barspoon

Citrus juicer

Shot glass

Collins glass

Coupe glass

Highball glass

Martini glass

Copita glass

Poco grande glass

Margarita glass

Red wine glass

White wine glass

Flute glass

Beer mug

Coffee mug

STOCKING THE CABINET

- Baileys Original Irish Cream
- Banana liqueur
- Beer
- Bitters (angostura)
- Blueberry liqueur
- Bourbon
- Brandy (unflavored, apricot)
- Campari
- Champagne
- Cider
- Cognac
- Cointreau
- Curaçao (blue, orange)
- Drambuie
- Flavored vodka (vanilla, blueberry, whipped cream)
- Fruit juices
- Gin
- Ginger ale
- Ginger beer
- Grenadine
- Jägermeister
- Kahlúa
- Malibu rum
- Peanut butter whiskey
- Port wine
- Prosecco
- Raspberry liqueur
- Red wine
- Rosé
- Rum (dark, light)
- Sake (dry)
- Schlitz Malt Liquor
- Schnapps (apple, blueberry, peach)
- Scotch whisky
- Southern Comfort
- St~Germain
- Tequila
- Triple sec
- Vermouth (dry, sweet)
- Vodka
- Whiskey
- White wine

1936 — 1959

Buddy Holly's
AMERICAN PIE

SERVES 1

Buddy Holly set the framework for the iconic rock sound of two guitars, bass, and drums. In his brief career as a singer-songwriter, both solo and as a member of the Crickets, Holly would score several major hits, including "That'll Be the Day" and "Peggy Sue," both released in 1957.

The Lubbock, Texas-born Holly was a churchgoing youth respectful of adults. He smoked only when his mother wasn't around and enjoyed the occasional bootleg beer,[1] but his drinking is believed to have been in moderation. Whether that was because alcohol was hard to find in his hometown so he never acquired a taste for it; because he suffered from an ulcer that alcohol inflamed, as was rumored, because his Baptist values opposed drinking; or because he was required to abide by the rules of the Crickets' manager, Norman Petty, who opposed drinking, is debated.[2]

Holly's life was cut short at age twenty-two, when the small plane he was flying in with fellow rock pioneers Ritchie Valens and J. P. Richardson (the Big Bopper) and their pilot crashed on the way to a concert Holly was scheduled to perform in. In 1971, singer-songwriter Don McLean released "American Pie," which immortalized the tragic event and the impact it had on the music world. The eight-minute song became a huge hit and even today continues to be a staple of rock radio.

Borrowing inspiration from the song, enjoy a classic American pie cocktail. Prepare it virgin, as Holly likely would have, or kick it up a notch if you're donning your dancing shoes and digging some rhythm and blues.

1 ½ ounces bourbon (optional)

½ ounce apple schnapps or apple juice

½ ounce Giffard Crème de Myrtille blueberry liqueur or ¼ cup blended blueberries

¾ ounce sweetened cranberry juice

¼ ounce lime juice, freshly squeezed

Apple wedge for garnishing

Shake all ingredients, except garnish, with ice in a cocktail shaker and strain into a chilled collins glass. Garnish with the apple wedge.

Jimi Hendrix's
PURPLE HAZE

⚡ **SERVES 1**

Who can forget the wake-up call that Jimi Hendrix gave at Woodstock in 1969, with an electrifying performance of "The Star-Spangled Banner" played on his electric guitar? No one could coax unusual sounds out of their guitar quite like the self-taught Hendrix. His short career saw a wealth of collaborations with other musicians and a pivotal role as the star member of the Jimi Hendrix Experience. By 1969 Hendrix was the world's highest-paid rock musician—an astounding title for a black American whose rise to fame coincided with the civil rights movement. Today he is best remembered for hits such as "Purple Haze" (1967), "Voodoo Child (Slight Return)" (1968), which showcased hard, psychedelic sounds, and "All Along the Watchtower" (1968), which was written and first recorded by Bob Dylan.

For insight into how Hendrix courted the muse, we can look to Leon Hendrix's book on his brother Jimi, in which Leon recalled that Jimi "always made sure a bottle of Johnnie Walker Red was backstage."[3] Sadly, Hendrix struggled with drug and alcohol abuse during his short life and when he died, at age twenty-seven, it was following the overuse of sleeping pills. This tasty tribute to the music legend should, in his honor, be consumed in moderation. Hendrix himself would likely have enjoyed the whisky straight-up, but try this version for a purple haze rendition.

1 ounce Johnnie Walker Red Label Scotch whisky

2 ounces cranberry juice

½ ounce Bols blue curaçao liqueur

Blueberries for garnishing

Fill a cocktail shaker with ice. Pour all ingredients except garnish in and then shake. Strain into a chilled martini glass filled with ice. Garnish with the blueberries.

Janis Joplin's
SOUTHERN NECTAR

SERVES 1

"Playing isn't necessarily about happiness. But it's just about letting yourself feel all those things that you have already on the inside of you, but you're all the time trying to push them aside because they don't make for polite conversation." —Janis Joplin

Janis Joplin was the queen of psychedelic soul music—a singer-songwriter whose distinctive, raspy voice fronted the band Big Brother and the Holding Company before she embarked on a solo career. Joplin's short but brilliant career would produce such hits as "Me and Bobby McGee" (1971) and stunning covers of "Piece of My Heart" (1968), an Aretha

Franklin song, and "Ball and Chain" (1967), which was originally written and produced by Big Mama Thornton.

Joplin was an unapologetic lover of the whiskey liqueur Southern Comfort. There are many photos of her onstage swigging from a bottle of SoCo, and she regularly spoke about how she enjoyed the drink. One time while inebriated, she smashed a bottle of SoCo into Jim Morrison's head. Rather than make him angry, this act reportedly made Morrison more interested in her—and it garnered loads of press.[4] As a way of saying thank you for all the free publicity, Southern Comfort sent Joplin a full-length lynx fur coat.

While Joplin was known to drink Southern Comfort straight, the Texas-born legend would likely have enjoyed this sweet nectar as well.[5] Do keep in mind that Joplin struggled with addiction and just one of these concoctions is enough to channel the music legend.

2 ounces Southern Comfort
whiskey liqueur

2 ounces apple juice

2 ounces cranberry juice

Lime wedge for garnishing

Combine all ingredients except
garnish in an ice-filled collins
glass and garnish with the lime
wedge. Enjoy while seated at a
window looking at the rain.

1943 — 1971

Jim Morrison's
BOILERMAKER

SERVES 1

"I see myself as a huge fiery comet, a shooting star. Everyone
stops, points up and gasps, 'Oh, look at that!' Then—whoosh,
and I'm gone . . . and they'll never see anything like it ever again."
—Jim Morrison

"**W**ell, I'll tell you a story of whiskey and mystics and
men" begins the Doors' song "Whiskey, Mystics and
Men" (1969), belted out in Jim Morrison's hypnotic, baritone
voice. Morrison, a superb poet and songwriter, was a master
lyricist and produced or coproduced such classics as "Light
My Fire" (1967), "Roadhouse Blues" (1970), and "L.A. Woman"

(1971). But while succinct in his lyrics and poems, Morrison was known to indulge in drugs, which would lead to his early death, and alcohol. His favorite drinks were reportedly Jack Daniel's whiskey, Chivas Regal Scotch whisky, and beer. On drinking, he once said, "You don't know where you're going to end up the next day. It could work out good or it could be disastrous. It's like the throw of the dice."[6]

The boilermaker is an easy-to-make drink: a beer and a shot of whiskey. It's a mix of two brews Morrison often—perhaps too often—partook in. Enjoy, and see if this concoction unleashes your inner poet or rock god.

1 ½ ounces
Jack Daniel's Old
No. 7 whiskey

12 ounces beer of choice

Pour the beer into a chilled beer mug. Add the whiskey and stir. Let the drink light your fire.

1915 — 1973

Sister Rosetta Tharpe's
BROWN DERBY

SERVES 1

No celebration of rock musicians would be complete without paying homage to Sister Rosetta Tharpe. One of the earliest influencers of rock and roll, Sister Rosetta helped inspire Elvis Presley, Little Richard, Chuck Berry, Johnny Cash, and others and laid the foundation for the rock music we know today. Among her hit songs are "Rock Me" (1938), "This Train" (1939), and "Strange Things Happening Every Day" (1944).

Sister Rosetta was born in Arkansas and grew up attending a Pentecostal church that encouraged musical expression, and she established her musical roots in gospel songs. At twenty-three she began recording professionally, singing and playing guitar, even though it was widely considered a man's instrument. Her style would fuse gospel and early rock tunes, a move that turned off some of her churchgoing fans but brought her a wider secular audience. During World War II, she would perform for black soldiers and acquire fame as gospel's first superstar. Later, she would delight fans by having her third wedding on the baseball field of Griffith Stadium in Washington, DC, and then performing for an audience filling the stadium. A queer black woman who became a superstar in the face of racism and sexism, Sister Rosetta would sometimes be turned away by segregated restaurants while her white male backup singers would be served instead.

According to biographer Gayle Wald, although Sister Rosetta had been raised to regard drinking alcohol as sinful, she would treat herself to a "nip now and then."[7] Her friend Roxie shared, "We weren't drunkards, but if we wanted a drink, we would take one."[8] It's not known what Sister Rosetta's drink of choice was, but it is known that in her later years she shared her belief that everyone should be drinking grapefruit juice as a cure for diabetes. On this, Wald theorized, "perhaps because she imagined the acidity of the bitter liquid would counterbalance the 'sweetness' in her blood."[9] Of course this was misguided, but to channel Sister Rosetta a grapefruit juice–based concoction fits the bill. We think she would have liked a brown derby, a cocktail developed in the 1930s that celebrates the fusion of grapefruit, bourbon, and honey notes—strong but sweet, just like Sister Rosetta.

| 1 ounce grapefruit juice | ½ ounce honey syrup | Grapefruit slice for garnishing |

1 ½ ounces bourbon

Mix all ingredients except garnish with ice in a cocktail shaker until well chilled. Strain into a coupe glass and garnish with the grapefruit slice.

1935 — 1977

Elvis Presley's
BANANA PEANUT BUTTER SHOT

SERVES 1

E lvis Presley was the king of rock and roll—the best-selling solo music artist of all time whose hip-shaking performances delighted fans worldwide and whose fresh vocals and impressive range delivered such rhythmic classics as "Hound Dog" (1956), "Love Me Tender" (1956), and "Are You Lonesome Tonight?" (1960), forever changing the nature of pop culture.

Onstage Presley had to be on his game, but behind closed doors, he liked to relax and indulge. It's been reported that in his Graceland mansion, he enjoyed southern foods, particularly meatloaf, fried chicken, and mac and cheese. According to his ex-wife, Priscilla Presley, Elvis was a creature of habit with his food and loved meatloaf and mashed potatoes so much that he once ate them for dinner every day for six months.[10]

Another of Presley's favorite foods, according to his personal chef, Mary Jenkins Langston, was fried peanut butter and banana sandwiches. Langston once revealed, "He said that the only thing in life he got any enjoyment out of was eating." Elaborating on the PB&Bs another time, she said: "If he wanted them in the morning when he woke up, I would have to fix 'em. If he wanted them at two o'clock in the morning, I would have to still fix them .... He wanted them real rich .... It'd be just floating in butter. You'd turn it and turn it and turn it until all the butter was soaked up. That's when he liked it."[11]

Presley's indulgence in food is likely what led to his vast weight gain in the years prior to his death, as it's believed he typically drank in moderation. The banana peanut butter shot presents the taste of the king's favorite meal in drink form.[12] Maintain a balanced diet, but indulge with this on occasion when you feel that hound dog need to shake, rattle, and roll.

1 ounce peanut butter whiskey	1 ounce banana liqueur	Bacon or fried banana slice for garnishing (optional)
1 ounce Irish cream		

Combine peanut butter whiskey, Irish cream, banana liqueur, and ice in a cocktail shaker and shake to mix and chill. Strain into a shot glass and garnish with a slice of bacon or fried banana.

John Lennon's
BRANDY ALEXANDER

SERVES 1

Legendary singer, songwriter, and peace activist John Lennon cofounded the Beatles in 1960 with Paul McCartney, George Harrison, and Ringo Starr and soon after ascended to rock royalty, responsible for such timeless hits as "Strawberry Fields Forever" (1967), "Let It Be" (1970), and "Imagine" (1971).

In public, Lennon was composed, but his personal life did allow for the occasional indulgence, particularly with his favorite cocktail, the brandy Alexander. Lennon was introduced to the drink on March 12, 1974, during his so-called "lost week-end"—a supposed weekend away from Yoko Ono that turned into eighteen months apart, during which Lennon caroused, raised hell, and had a well-publicized relationship with May Pang, a music executive and assistant to Lennon and Yoko. On that Tuesday night, Lennon and singer-songwriter Harry Nilsson were thrown out of West Hollywood's Troubadour club for "relentlessly heckling" the folk-singing duo the Smothers Brothers, who were performing.[13] Lennon later reminisced, "I got drunk and shouted. It was the first night I drank brandy Alexanders, which is brandy and milk, folks. . . . I usually have somebody there who says, 'Okay, Lennon, shut up,' and they take it, but I didn't have anybody around me to say shut up and I just went on and on."[14] Lennon and Nilsson would end up drunkenly looking to fight, and later, sobered up and back to their old selves, sending flowers and an apology to the Smothers Brothers.

The brandy Alexander tastes like a milkshake and its sweetness delighted Lennon, a chocolate lover. Try it yourself, but avoid throwing punches and, as Lennon sings in "Instant Karma!" (1970), we'll "all shine on."

1 ½ ounces brandy

1 ½ ounces crème de cacao

1 ½ ounces heavy whipping cream

¼ teaspoon cocoa powder

Maraschino cherries for garnishing

Combine all ingredients except garnish with several ice cubes in a cocktail shaker and shake vigorously for 30 seconds. Strain into a collins glass and garnish with the cherries.

1945 — 1981

Bob Marley's
JAMAICAN IRISH MOSS

SERVES 1

J amaican singer-songwriter Bob Marley captured the hearts of fans worldwide with his blend of reggae, ska, and rocksteady. Marley would also become a fierce social leader, a devoted Rastafarian, an advocate for Pan-Africanism, and according to *GQ*, "an underrated style god."[15] By the time of his death at just thirty-six, he had produced such iconic, rhythmic hits as "Get Up, Stand Up" (1973), "No Woman, No Cry" (1975), and "Redemption Song" (1980). Today, his albums have sold more than seventy million copies.

Marley's devotion to Rastafarianism was linked to his regular use of marijuana, but a disdain for drinking alcohol. Asked about this, he once told a reporter: "Alcohol make you drunk, man. It don't make you meditate, it just make you drunk. . . . Herb is more a consciousness."[16] He did, however, enjoy earthy juices. In one scene from Timothy White's book *Catch a Fire: The Life of Bob Marley*, White describes how Marley and his housemates would jog to a local market every Sunday, where Marley would select the carrots, soursop, and Irish Moss—"a type of seaweed used for making a sweet, gelatinous drink believed to encourage the libido"—that would be used in the housemates' juices during the week.[17]

To channel Marley, enjoy your own Jamaican Irish moss. Set Marley's tunes to play on repeat as you carefully prepare the star ingredient and keep in mind that as the drink is a reported aphrodisiac, it may be best enjoyed on a romantic night in. Enjoy it virgin as Marley would have, or add an extra kick with the rum.

2 ounces Irish moss, thoroughly washed

4 cups coconut milk, cold, divided

¼ cup ground flaxseed

6 strands isinglass

3 pieces gum arabic

¾ cup agave

2 teaspoons vanilla extract

1 teaspoon ground nutmeg

Ground cinnamon, to taste

1 ounce Jamaican white rum (optional)

In a blender combine Irish moss with 2 cups of the coconut milk and ice until the moss has been well pulverized, then set aside. Warm 2 cups water with the remaining 2 cups coconut milk in a saucepan set over medium heat. Add ⅓ cup of the Irish moss and coconut milk mixture and the flaxseed, isinglass, and gum arabic to the saucepan and bring to a boil. Once boiling, lower the heat to a simmer and cook for 30 minutes, stirring regularly. After 30 minutes, add agave, vanilla, nutmeg, and cinnamon, and cook over low heat for an additional 10 minutes, stirring occasionally. Remove from the heat and strain out any moss. Cool in the refrigerator for 3 hours, then remove and stir in the rum, if using. Serve cold in a collins glass with a sprinkle of cinnamon.

1946 — 1991

Freddie Mercury's
BOHEMIAN
VODKA TONIC

SERVES 1

"I won't be a rock star. I will be a legend." —Freddie Mercury

Freddie Mercury, the front man for the band Queen, mesmerized audiences with his distinctive, operatic voice and flamboyant stage presence. The band's dramatic hit "Bohemian Rhapsody" (1975) regularly ranks among the top five rock songs of all time even today, and with other hits like "Don't Stop Me Now" (1978) and "Another One Bites the Dust" (1980), Queen is responsible for some of the most streamed rock songs of all time.

According to Peter "Phoebe" Freestone, Mercury's longtime personal assistant, the rock star would regularly enjoy a cup of Earl Grey tea three or four times a day, and when he was looking for something harder, he'd go for champagne, Swiss wine from Lavaux, or a vodka tonic made from Stolichnaya vodka, known as Stoli, and Schweppes tonic.[18] In one memorable story recounted by Queen guitarist Brian May, Mercury's health had deteriorated toward the end of his life such that May wasn't sure if he would be able to record the song "The Show Must Go On" (1991), but Mercury relied on his drink of choice and pulled through. May recalled, "I said, 'Fred, I don't know if this is going to be possible to sing.' And he went, 'I'll fucking do it, darling'—vodka down—and went in and killed it."[19]

In 2014, surviving members of Queen paired up with Stoli to create Killer Queen vodka, with May revealing, "Freddie loved vodka and used to carry a dry ice cooler full of vodka with him on tour."[20] The specialty drink is no longer produced, but like Freddie, we think Stoli's classic vodka manages just fine. Use their blueberry flavor for a flavorful bohemian flair, as Freddie likely would have wanted.

2 ounces Stoli Blueberi vodka	5 ounces Schweppes tonic water	Lemon wedge for garnishing

Fill a highball glass with ice, then add the vodka and top off with tonic water. Garnish with the lemon wedge and stir. Channel Freddie by sipping gracefully while donning a glittery military jacket studded with epaulets, or go all out with a burgundy cape and crown. Release your inner queen.

1940 ———————— 1993

Frank Zappa's
COFFEE AND FRIED SPAGHETTI

SERVES 1

"I like fried spaghetti. I like Fried Anything. Whatever it is, FRY IT." —Frank Zappa

The innovative, outside-the-box musician Frank Zappa began his rise to fame in the 1960s, as a singer and guitarist for the band that would become Mothers of Invention. Zappa's music would come to incorporate elements of rock, jazz, blues, doo-wop, and more, with Zappa often taking an experimental approach and overlaying his work with satirical, abstract, and humorous lyrics. He would also become politically active, taking an anti-authority stance and testifying in Congress to oppose censorship. Among his top songs are "Cosmik Debris" (1974), "Joe's Garage" (1979), part of a three-part rock opera, and "Valley Girl" (1982), which featured Zappa's then-fourteen-year-old daughter, Moon.

Although Zappa's wild character and music often left audiences believing he must have been indulging in stimulants, he disliked drugs and alcohol. According to Zappa's memoir, after drinking some beer he once felt that his "stomach swelled up as if the Alien was going to pop out" and he "fell off the chair writhing in agony—cursing the Miller High Life company."[21] Zappa did, however, regularly enjoy coffee and cigarettes; according to his brother Bob, Zappa was "always smoking, always drinking coffee."[22] With that in mind, skip the alcohol when deciding on a brew to channel Zappa and instead go for a solid cup of coffee. For best effect, pair it with Zappa's favorite food, fried spaghetti, which the artist believed was best consumed for breakfast.[23]

COFFEE

1 mug brewed coffee

FRIED SPAGHETTI

2 ounces spaghetti noodles
2 ounces tomato sauce

Pour coffee into a coffee mug and set aside. Cook spaghetti according to package directions, then transfer cooked noodles to a skillet set over medium heat. Add tomato sauce and fry noodles to taste, then transfer to a plate. Enjoy coffee and spaghetti while watching the sun rise.

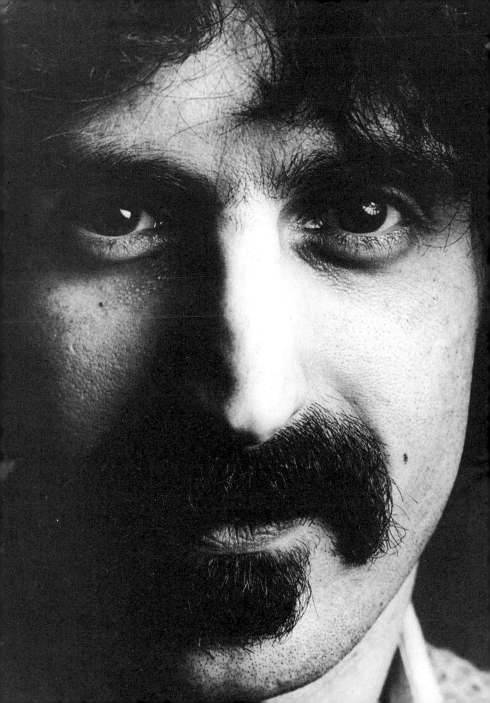

1942 — 1995

Jerry Garcia's
RUM SCREWDRIVER

SERVES 1

Considered one of the greatest guitarists of all time, Jerry Garcia was a founder of the Grateful Dead and a front man for the band throughout its thirty years, as well as the star of the Jerry Garcia Band. His contributions would lead the Grateful Dead to sell millions of albums, attributable to hits such as "Dark Star" (1969), written by Robert Hunter and composed by Garcia, "Friend of the Devil" (1970), written by Garcia and John Dawson, and "Uncle John's Band," written by Garcia and Hunter. The Dead's fusion of traditional rock sounds with psychedelic rock, bluegrass, and more would prove to resonate well with the counterculture youth of the seventies and eighties and spawn a devoted following of self-proclaimed Dead Heads—and according to the band's website, Garcia's "warm, charismatic personality . . . earned him the affection of millions of Dead Heads."[24]

Unfortunately, while Garcia was widely beloved, personal demons led to long-standing addictions to heroin, cocaine, cigarettes, and food, and resulting health problems. While we're not certain what drink Garcia most enjoyed partaking in, a backstage rider from a 1976 show of the Jerry Garcia Band shows that one pint of "Bacardí Lite Rum" (Bacardí's white rum) and four quarts of orange juice (no sugar added) were a requirement.[25] With that in mind, it's easy to envision the charismatic performer sipping a rum screwdriver before one of his mesmerizing guitar riffs. To channel Garcia, let loose to some of his top tunes and sip this sweet treat.

| 2 ounces Bacardí white rum | 2 ounces orange juice, freshly squeezed | Orange slice for garnishing |

Mix rum and juice together in an ice-filled highball glass. Garnish with the orange slice. If enjoying before a night out, remember to get home before daylight so you might get some sleep tonight.

Tip: The Jerry Garcia Band rider also required bacon, lettuce, and tomato sandwiches and "good cheeseburgers." Have one of these at the ready to accompany this cocktail to further channel Garcia.

1974 — 1996

The Ramones'
TANQUERAY
AND TONIC

SERVES 1

Founded in New York City in 1974, the Ramones were a genre-defining punk rock group comprised of highly talented, energized musicians known to rebel and play tricks on one another and other musicians. None of the band members were biologically related, but all took on stage names ending in Ramone. The original lineup and founding members were singer Joey Ramone, bassist Dee Dee Ramone, guitarist Johnny Ramone, and drummer Tommy Ramone, and later bassist C. J. Ramone and drummers Marky Ramone, Richie Ramone, and

Elvis Ramone joined the group. Among their greatest hits are "Blitzkrieg Bop" (1976), "Beat on the Brat" (1976), and "I Wanna Be Sedated" (1978).

The craziness that defined the band's way of being included such impossible-to-make-up stories as Johnny "stealing" Joey's girlfriend, which led to the two hardly speaking for fifteen years; that the band's preshow ritual was to gorge on super spicy curry, which inevitably led to at least one member throwing up during each performance; and that one of the band members urinated in a beer bottle and tricked Johnny Rotten of the Sex Pistols into drinking it.

Each band member had a different relationship with drugs and alcohol, with Johnny very conservative with his drinking and other band members more prone to indulge. What is known is that their song "Somebody Put Something in My Drink" (1986), written by Richie, was based on his drink once being spiked with LSD. According to the lyrics: "Somebody put something in my drink . . . Tanqueray and tonic's my favorite drink. I don't like anything colored pink. That just stinks." To channel the band, make sure to skip all pink additions and simply enjoy the drink as it was intended: simple and clear in color.

2 ounces Tanqueray
London Dry Gin

4 ounces
tonic water

Lime wedge
for garnishing

Fill a highball glass with ice, add gin and tonic water, and stir. Garnish with the lime wedge. Sip while letting loose and rocking hard. "*Babam-ba-baba . . . hey, oh, let's go.*"

1952 — 2002

Joe Strummer's
HARD CIDER

SERVES 1

Cofounder, singer, and guitarist for the Clash before his successful solo career, Joe Strummer was a pioneer of punk rock. The members of the Clash performed together from 1976 to 1986, and when they were later inducted into the Rock and Roll Hall of Fame, they were called one of the "most explosive and exciting bands in rock and roll history ... [whose] up-tempo punk-rock manifestos were unleashed with pure adrenaline and total conviction."[26] After the Clash disbanded, Strummer performed solo and created the group the Mescaleros. Among Strummer's most memorable songs are "(White Man) In Hammersmith Palais" (1978), "London Calling" (1979), and "Rock the Casbah" (1982).

A wild child, Strummer was known to enjoy his drinking, partying, and troublemaking, which led to the occasional arrest. In one interview he shared how he ran the Paris Marathon three times and his training regime was to "not run a single step at least four weeks before the race . . . [and to] drink ten pints of beer the night before the race."[27]

In addition to enjoying his beer, Strummer was known to have a special affinity for hard cider and regularly visited Wilkins Cider Farm in the UK. Reportedly, his definition of happiness was "Chilling in Somerset with a flagon of Wilkins Farmhouse Cider."[28] According to Roger Wilkins, whose family owned the cider farm: "Joe used to love it here. He was a regular. He'd come down and sit in the barn for a few hours and drink and smoke. I'd cut him some cheese and bring it out to him. He used to describe it as a 'bit of heaven.'"[29]

To channel Strummer, kick back with a hard cider. For added effect, pair with a side of cheese, like Wilkins's cheddar or stilton specialties.

| 12 ounces Wilkins Farmhouse Cider or other dry cider, chilled | Cheddar or stilton cheese for pairing (optional) |

Pour cider into a goblet and pair with a serving of cheese. Sip quietly in a barn during lunchtime while writing lyrics and planning an explosive set for the night.

1932 – – 2003

Johnny Cash's
DARK 'N' STORMY

SERVES 1

With his smooth bass-baritone voice and catchy, memorable lyrics, Johnny Cash overcame a troubled childhood, including the loss of his brother, and rose to fame in the mid-1950s. His songs would fuse elements of rock, rockabilly, country, blues, and gospel and lead to his entry into three music halls of fame and a massive devoted fan base. Among his hits are "I Walk the Line" (1956), "Folsom Prison Blues" (1968), and "A Boy Named Sue" (1968).

Much to the delight of fans, Cash would propose to his second wife, entertainer June Carter, onstage (after her refusal on many prior occasions) and the two would embark on a love story for the ages. Unfortunately, Cash would suffer for many years from an addiction to amphetamines and barbiturates that he would chase with alcohol, before Carter helped him overcome his addiction. According to Cash, "Amphetamines are hard to angle, and once you're into them to any extent you find out very quickly that you have a pressing need for other chemicals. I soon had to drink alcohol, usually wine or beer, to take the edge off my high."[30]

To channel Cash, stick to the alcohol and forgo the pills. If a beer alone won't do the trick, we recommend a single dark 'n' stormy. Cash was nicknamed the "man in black" and this dark ginger beer–based concoction is certainly reminiscent of him.

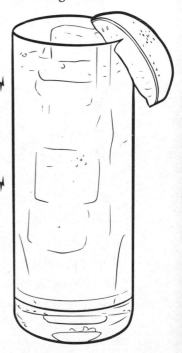

3 ounces ginger beer	½ ounce lime juice, freshly squeezed
2 ounces dark rum	Lime wedge for garnishing

Mix beer, rum, and lime juice in an ice-filled collins glass. Garnish with the lime wedge. Drink while crooning deep, soulful tunes.

Michael Jackson's
JESUS JUICE

SERVES 1

Michael Jackson was one of the most significant artists of the twentieth century. He began his career as a child performer in his family's Jackson 5 band and would embark on a solo career in 1971. His incredible dance-friendly, mood-boosting hits would define him as a global superstar and one of the all-time best-selling artists, with more than 400 million albums sold worldwide and fifteen Grammy Awards to his name. Classic MJ songs include "Don't Stop 'Til You Get Enough" (1979), "Thriller" (1982), and "Billie Jean" (1983). Jackson would also be responsible for popularizing the iconic dance move the moonwalk.

But while Jackson would become one of our most significant cultural icons and the face of super-stardom, he was not without controversy, and there are many questions surrounding what went on behind closed doors at his Neverland Ranch. What is well-reported is that the star frequently enjoyed wine—perhaps occasionally overindulging, as the godfather of his children reportedly shared that Jackson was drinking up to six bottles of wine a day in the weeks leading up to his death.[31] It's also been widely reported that the star often drank white wine out of Diet Coke cans to disguise what he was indulging in, and that he would call it his "Jesus Juice." When he drank red wine, he called it "Jesus's Blood."[32] Referring to the wine, he reportedly said, "Jesus drank it, so it must be good."[33] It's believed Jackson even considered turning part of his ranch into a small vineyard.[34]

12-ounce can Diet Coke (not for drinking)
12 ounces white wine of choice, chilled

Pour out the soda from the can, rinse with water, then fill with the wine. Enjoy while practicing your moonwalk. Repeat until you get enough.

1956 — — 2010

Simon and Garfunkel's
VODKA GIMLET

SERVES 1

Paul Simon and Art Garfunkel combined their creative genius in 1956 to create the band Simon and Garfunkel. With their unique folk-rock sound, epic harmonizing, powerful blend of acoustic and electric guitars, and catchy lyrics, the New York–born duo would become one of the most successful bands of the 1960s. Among their greatest hits are "The Sound of Silence" (1965), "The Boxer" (1969), and "Bridge over Troubled Water" (1970). In total their albums have sold more than 100 million copies.

Simon and Garfunkel would play together until 1970 and reunite for shared performances over the years that followed, in addition to launching solo careers. Their relationship, however, was known to be a turbulent one, with artistic differences causing recurring disagreements—troubled waters, so to speak. Still, there was magic in what they created together. While the musicians are fiercely private and their drinks of choice are not known, we do know that drinking a "vodka and lime" was part of the lyrics of "A Hazy Shade of Winter" (1966), and we like to imagine the two rockers kicking back with one as they build a bridge and let their disagreements fall by the wayside.

2 ounces vodka

¾ ounce lime juice, freshly squeezed

½ ounce simple syrup

Lime wedge for garnishing

Mix vodka, lime juice, and simple syrup with ice in a cocktail shaker. Strain into a martini glass and garnish with the lime wedge. Make sure to turn up the Simon & Garfunkel tunes while enjoying and putting your own troubled waters behind you.

1983 — 2011

Amy Winehouse's
RICKSTACY

SERVES 1

With her remarkable husky voice and three-octave vocal range, singer-songwriter Amy Winehouse shot to global fame and became a rock icon. The London-born artist would score six Grammy Awards during her short career and produce such chart-topping hits as "Back to Black" (2006), "Rehab" (2006), and "Love Is a Losing Game" (2007).

Unfortunately, while Winehouse was talented beyond measure and an inspiration to a generation of girls, she battled personal demons and suffered from drug and alcohol addictions, which would lead to her untimely death at just twenty-seven. To honor Winehouse, make sure to enjoy this sweet drink in moderation—one per person is plenty. The drink, called a rickstacy, is widely believed to have been her favorite cocktail, and as legend has it, one she acquired a taste for at the Hawley Arms pub, which was among the pubs she frequently visited.

1 ½ ounces vodka

½ ounce
banana liqueur

½ ounce Southern
Comfort whiskey
liqueur

½ ounce
Baileys Original
Irish Cream

Combine all ingredients in a chilled cocktail shaker, shaking well. Pour into an ice-filled poco grande glass. To best channel Winehouse, enjoy while sporting a beehive and heavy black eyeliner and singing deep, soul-tugging lyrics.

1963 — — 2012

Whitney Houston's
CHAMPAGNE

SERVES 1

The legendary singer Whitney Houston had an extraordinary five-octave vocal range, compelling stage presence, and fierce determination that helped her overcome prejudices and challenges. The result was that Houston would become one of the best-selling recording artists of all time, with hits including "How Will I Know" (1985), "I Wanna Dance with Somebody (Who Loves Me)" (1987), and "I Will Always Love You" (1992), her version of a Dolly Parton song, which she recorded for the 1992 film *The Bodyguard* and which would spend a record-breaking fourteen weeks at No. 1 on *Billboard*'s Hot 100 list.

But while Houston was a powerhouse musician, her personal struggles included a turbulent relationship with her husband of many years, Bobby Brown, and problems with drug abuse. She would tell Oprah that while she wasn't a big drinker, she and Brown indulged in cocaine and marijuana.[35] Still, she did enjoy a drink from time to time, and others have shared memories of her enjoying champagne. In Ian Halperin's book *Whitney & Bobbi Kristina*, he writes about a time when "Whitney was visibly drunk—having guzzled significant quantities of tequila and champagne"[36]—and there are multiple photos of the singer with a glass of bubbly. In Houston's honor, be sure to drink in moderation, enjoying the celebratory beverage but not to excess.

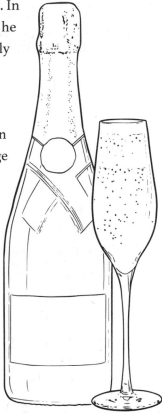

6 ounces champagne, chilled

Pour champagne into a tilted champagne flute. For best effects, sip while sporting a power blazer with shoulder pads, singing your heart out, and dancing with somebody who loves you—that's the Whitney way. *"Oooh . . . Don't you wanna dance? Say you wanna dance, uh-huh. . . !"*

Lemmy Kilmister's
JACK AND COKE

SERVES 1

"A kid once said to me, 'Do you get hangovers?' I said, 'To get hangovers you have to stop drinking.'" —Lemmy Kilmister

Motörhead was once described as a "blitzkrieg-fast band of outlaws that bridged early punk and metal with a hopped-up aural ferocity and unrelenting bad attitude."[37] Their leader, the singer and bassist known as Lemmy, was the personification of the band and its hard-rock lifestyle and helped Motörhead shoot to fame with such memorable hits as "Overkill" (1979), "Bomber" (1979), and "Ace of Spades" (1980).

Lemmy professed a love for Jack Daniel's whiskey, particularly when consumed as part of a Jack and Coke cocktail. He admitted to drinking a bottle of the whiskey a day for many years and only somewhat curtailing this habit when he recognized that the Coke wasn't good for his diabetes.[38] He then swapped his go-to cocktail for vodka and orange juice.[39]

Tony Iommi, the guitarist for Black Sabbath who toured with Motörhead dozens of times, confirmed Lemmy's penchant for whiskey, saying: "There was never any food. It was always two bottles of Jack Daniel's, two bottles of vodka, a couple of cases of beer. And that was them; that's the way they were."[40] In fact, so known was Lemmy's drink of choice that after the musician passed away, fans campaigned to have a Jack and Coke officially renamed a Lemmy.

2 ounces Jack Daniel's Old No. 7 whiskey

Dash bitters

Coca-Cola for topping

Fill a highball glass three-quarters full with ice. Pour whiskey over the ice, stir in bitters, and top with Coke. Drink fast while rocking hard and raising hell.

David Bowie's
ZIGGY STARDUST
BOMBAY SAPPHIRE
MARTINI

SERVES 1

A rock and roll chameleon, singer, songwriter, musician, performance artist, and fashion icon, David Bowie embraced musical styles ranging from the psychedelia of "Space Oddity" (1969) to the R & B groove of "Young Americans" (1975) and the cutting-edge techno of "I'm Afraid of Americans" (1997), and everything in between. A poster child for misfits and those looking to express their individuality,

78

Bowie lived an eclectic life, taking on such personas as Ziggy Stardust, Aladdin Sane, and the Thin White Duke, with those personas often blurring the lines between his personal and professional lives.

But while Bowie may have been larger than life, his drink of choice was clean and neat, and he was known for regularly ordering a gin martini made with Bombay Sapphire gin.[41] For a Ziggy Stardust twist of pizazz, swap a martini's traditional olive for a slice of grapefruit and a sprig of rosemary.

¼ ounce dry vermouth

2 ounces Bombay Sapphire gin

Grapefruit wedge for garnishing

Rosemary sprig for garnishing

Mix vermouth and gin with ice in a cocktail shaker, then strain into a martini glass. Garnish with the grapefruit and rosemary. For best effects, sip while dressed in an artfully tailored suit and lounging beside a haunted pool.

1958 — 2016

Prince's
PURPLE RAIN
SANGRIA

SERVES 8

The multitalented rock legend Prince was a singer, song-writer, guitarist, keyboardist, drummer, and bassist whose mix of up-tempo and soulful tunes made use of his remarkable vocal range and incorporated elements of R & B, funk, and much more. A prolific musician who would produce thirty-nine albums over his career and whose albums have sold more than 150 million copies, Prince's songs include such classics as "Purple Rain" (1984), "When Doves Cry" (1984), and "Let's Go Crazy" (1984). These three hits all appeared on Prince's *Purple Rain* album and the color purple became associated with the star.

Prince became a Jehovah's Witness in 2011 and he embraced the religion's belief that alcohol should only be consumed in moderation. Reportedly, he occasionally drank red wine but never beer, and thought Scotch was "disgusting."[42] To channel Prince, enjoy this sangria cocktail in his favorite hue. Keep in mind that Prince's diet was vegan or vegetarian, so avoid indulging in animal products after—the rock god would not approve.

1 cup blackberries, sliced

1 cup blueberries, sliced

1 cup purple grapes, sliced

2 cups purple grape juice

750-milliliter bottle red wine

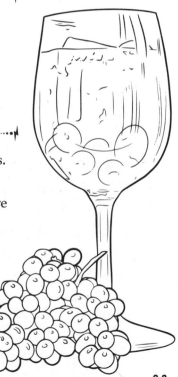

In a large pitcher, combine all ingredients. Stir while being careful not to injure the fruit. Refrigerate for at least 2 hours before serving. Enjoy in red wine glasses, while donning a sequined suit and ruffled blouse. Avoid any partaker having sorrow or pain while indulging; everyone should be smiling with the purple rain.

1926 — — 2017

Chuck Berry's
ORANGE BLOSSOM

SERVES 1

The great singer, songwriter, and guitarist Chuck Berry, often called the father of rock and roll, was the first musician to be inducted into the Rock and Roll Hall of Fame. Berry's rhythmic song "Maybellene" (1955) is considered to have been the first rock song, and he later scored dozens of hits, including "Roll Over Beethoven" (1956) and "Johnny B. Goode" (1958). On Berry's ninetieth birthday, he announced the upcoming release of his twentieth studio album. Posthumously for Berry, it would reach the UK's top-ten chart and be ranked forty-nine on the US Billboard 200 list.

As a teenager, Berry became sick after drinking a half-pint of whiskey and swore off drinking for the rest of his life.[43] But even without alcohol fueling his wild side, he had run-ins with the law several times throughout his life. In his memoir, he describes sex and women as his vices. He also shares his dietary preferences, including "orange juice all the time, anytime."[44]

In the song "Bring Another Drink" (1967), Berry sings about a party held "at the gin mill down the street" and that "The band was wailin' in the groove, 'Bring us all some juice.'" With his love for OJ, we're certain an orange blossom would have been flowing freely at this celebration. Enjoy the cocktail in its traditional form or prepare it virgin, as Berry would have taken it any time of day.

¾ ounce gin or ginger ale

¾ ounce sweet vermouth (optional)

1 ounce orange juice, freshly squeezed

Orange slice for garnishing

GINGER ALE

Combine all ingredients except garnish in a cocktail shaker with ice. Shake well and strain into a coupe glass. Garnish with the orange slice.

TIP: To channel Berry even further, enjoy with a side of soft vanilla pound cake or Dutch apple pie, Berry's preferred treats.[45]

Fats Domino's
COLD HEINEKEN AND RED BEANS

SERVES 1

The New Orleans–born singer, songwriter, and pianist Fats Domino was a pioneer of rock and roll, with his rhythm-and-blues-inflected tunes and catchy boogie-woogie piano playing capturing the respect of adoring fans nationwide. Domino's remarkable seventy-five years as a musician would lead to sales of more than sixty-five million albums and such hits as "Ain't That a Shame" (1955), "I'm In Love Again" (1956), and his cover of "Blueberry Hill" (1956), which would become his biggest hit.

Where Domino drew his strength and cheerful spirit from is unknown, but what is known is that he greatly enjoyed eating, drinking, and simply letting loose. Numerous sources have shared Domino's appreciation for simple things like a cold Heineken beer enjoyed on his New Orleans stoop. Recalling Domino returning back to New Orleans for the first time after Hurricane Katrina, a friend painted a picture, sharing: "It was a very heavy situation but we were sitting on the porch and he was having a cold Heineken. That was his favorite thing in the world."[46]

To channel the boogie-woogie legend, who Elvis Presley referred to as the "real king" of rock, enjoy a cold Heineken just as Domino would have. For good measure, add a side of cooked red beans to accompany the beer. Domino was known to travel with a hot plate and canned red beans so that he could "whip up some New Orleans-style food when the craving struck."[47]

12-ounce bottle
Heineken Original, chilled

Cooked red beans
for pairing (optional)

Pour chilled beer into a beer mug and enjoy with a side of cooked red beans. Sip while finding your thrill on Blueberry Hill as the wind in the willow plays love's sweet melody.

1942 — 2018

Aretha Franklin's
WHISKEY GINGER

SERVES 1

Singer, songwriter, pianist, and all-around tour de force Aretha Franklin has sold more than seventy-five million albums, and overcame multiple challenges and prejudices in her rise to fame. With her powerful voice, the queen of soul performed for more than sixty years, in the process earning a whopping forty-four Grammy nominations and eighteen wins, in addition to a Presidential Medal of Freedom and a wealth of other awards. Among her remarkable repertoire of hits are such music staples as "Respect" (1967), which utilized lyrics originally written by Otis Redding but reworked by Franklin,

"(You Make Me Feel Like) A Natural Woman" (1967), and "I Say a Little Prayer" (1968), which was also a cover redone by Franklin.

By every measure Franklin was a powerhouse, and some believe that it was the challenges she overcame that led to her success. And her challenges were great: beyond being a black woman in an industry dominated by white men, Franklin was the product of a difficult childhood marked by her mother's death followed by pregnancies as a preteen and teen. As an adult, it's known that Franklin often relied on drinking to help her get by. As the singer was fiercely private, little is known about her drink of choice. We do know, however, that in her lovely cover of "Drinking Again" (1964), she sings, "I ain't got nothing but a bottle of Seagram's" and that she had a fondness for ginger ale. Ginger ale was a part of some of her diets and was a requirement of her backstage rider.[48] Thus to channel the queen, try your hand at this concoction.

½ ounce Seagram's 7 Crown Blended Whiskey	½ ounce ginger ale	Lime wedge for garnishing

Combine whiskey and ginger ale in a highball glass filled with ice. Stir well and garnish with the lime wedge. For best results, turn the volume on your Aretha tunes up high and let loose when you sing, "*R-E-S-P-E-C-T*." Consider donning a sequined gown or feather boa for added drama.

1932 — 2020

Little Richard's
TUTTI FRUTTI

SERVES 1

Little Richard was one of the most influential musicians during the early days of rock and roll. The flamboyant and charismatic showman, known for his pounding piano fingers and joyous, inimitable "Wooo!," called himself the inventor and architect of rock and roll.[49] His career spanned seven decades, but his most seminal classics were produced during the mid-1950s, when he recorded such party-starting hits as "Tutti Frutti" (1955), "Lucille" (1957), and "Keep A-Knockin'" (1957).

Although Little Richard was sober for many years, early and late in his career he did have periods of extreme indulgence. If you're in a jamming, wop-bop-a-loo kind of mood, enjoy a Tutti Frutti cocktail, as the great architect likely would have during those years, or make the mocktail version that he would have preferred in his sober days.

½ ounce Malibu rum or grapefruit juice

½ ounce vodka (optional)

½ ounce peach schnapps or peach nectar

2 ½ ounces pineapple juice

Pineapple slice for garnishing

Pour all ingredients except garnish into an ice-filled cocktail shaker and shake well. Strain into a chilled collins glass and garnish with the pineapple slice. Enjoy with abandon, letting out a room shaking *"Wooo!"* after every few sips.

Jerry Lee Lewis's
WHISKEY TALKIN'

SERVES 1

A master pianist and singer-songwriter, Jerry Lee Lewis, nicknamed "the Killer," helped to define rock and roll. His unique renditions of "Great Balls of Fire" (1957) and "Whole Lotta Shakin' Goin' On" (1957), which paired wild piano tunes with catchy lyrics, became classics, and Lewis became notorious as a rock and roll wild man with his lifestyle choices and shocking activities, which included seven marriages (including one to a teenage cousin), an arrest outside Graceland for allegedly intending to shoot Elvis, Lewis's accidental shooting of his bass player in the chest, tax evasion, and indulgences in prescription drugs and sometimes whiskey.

Lewis's favorite whiskey was Calvert Extra and he was known to drink it straight. In *Jerry Lee Lewis: His Own Story*, Lewis shared: "I'd buy a fifth of Calvert Extra whiskey. And I'd keep it to myself—I hid it in my shaving kit." Lewis claims he drank the fifth over the course of a week.[50] Though the jury is still out on that, Lewis did eventually give up his "old friend Calvert whiskey,"[51] and today he's been clean for decades. If you're looking to channel the Killer during his heyday, indulge in Calvert Extra enjoyed neat.

1 ½ ounces Calvert Extra whiskey

Pour whiskey into a rocks glass and set atop the piano. Enjoy sips between songs.

Grace Slick's
MULLED WINE

SERVES 1

Known as the "acid queen," Grace Slick was a defining voice in the psychedelic rock scene of the sixties and seventies. Her music career launched in San Francisco in 1965 with the band the Great Society, for whom she composed the popular psychedelic song "White Rabbit" (1965). In 1966, she replaced the lead singer of the band Jefferson Airplane. With the new band Slick would become one of the most successful female performers of her time, working with Jefferson Airplane into the early 1970s and then forming the band Jefferson Starship. Among Slick's hits are such classics as "Somebody to

Love" (1967), "Mexico" (1970), and "Nothing's Gonna Stop Us Now" (1987).

A true counterculture presence, Slick was a friend and drinking buddy of Janis Joplin, attempted to spike President Richard Nixon's drink with LSD at a White House tea party, was the first person to use "the F-word" on American television, had songs banned because of drug references, and was arrested at least four times—for what she has referred to as a "TUI"—talking under the influence. We know at least one of these arrests was after an altercation instigated by wine, and given how frequently wine is featured in her memoir, it's probably safe to assume they all were.

In one scene of Slick's memoir, she paints a portrait of a day ending with "a late dinner by candlelight and congenial conversation with friends over a couple of mugs of mulled wine"[52]—and the appeal of this to her is clear. To channel the acid queen, then, take a go at a glass of this warming brew.

¾ cup red wine

1 tablespoon whiskey

1 tablespoon orange juice, freshly squeezed

½ teaspoon honey syrup

1 shake ground cloves

1 shake ground cinnamon

1 shake ground nutmeg

Orange slice for garnishing

Cinnamon stick for garnishing

Combine all ingredients except garnishes in a saucepan set over medium heat and bring to a boil. Once boiling, reduce heat to low and let simmer for 5 minutes. Pour into a mug and garnish with the orange slice and cinnamon stick. Drink while building dreams, cursing freely, and singing wildly, preferably by candlelight with friends. Nothing's gonna stop you now.

Tina Turner's
RED WINE AND
FINE CHOCOLATE

SERVES 1

Known as the queen of rock and roll, singer-songwriter
Tina Turner's extraordinary vocal range and powerful
stage presence have enthralled fans throughout her more than
fifty years as a performer. Turner's rise to fame was through
a partnership with her former husband Ike Turner, and
after the duo split she launched a successful solo career. The
winner of twelve Grammy Awards, Turner's hits include "River
Deep—Mountain High" (1966), a song she performed with Ike,
"What's Love Got to Do with It" (1984), which hit No. 1 on the

Billboard Hot 100 list, and "The Best" (1989). Altogether Turner has sold more than 100 million albums, making her one of the best-selling artists of all time.

Although Turner is a music legend who has battled demons in her personal life, she is not known to have suffered with addictions like so many other superstars; instead, she is known for being health conscious. In providing tips for how to stay healthy, she has shared the importance of consuming alcohol in moderation. One article on her diet notes her recommendation to "reduce your alcohol intake but you can allow yourself a small glass of red wine with dinner."[53] As to where else Turner might have allowed herself to indulge, we can find a hint in one of her backstage riders that required "good European chocolates" in addition to Snickers bars.[54] We like to imagine the queen wanted to give herself the option to go high- or lowbrow in her chocolate treat of the day.

To channel Turner, let yourself enjoy a glass of high-quality red wine with dinner and some good European chocolates. Consider enjoying while decked out in a sparkly mini dress or a sophisticated pantsuit.

5 ounces red wine

Good European
chocolates for pairing

Pour red wine into a red wine
glass and enjoy with a side
of the chocolates. Let the
luxurious flavors dance on your
taste buds and know that you
deserve this, because you're
simply the best.

1941

Bob Dylan's
BOURBON
SERVED NEAT

SERVES 1

With his unique blend of rock and folk music, singer, songwriter, and guitarist Bob Dylan has sold more than 125 million albums and won ten Grammy Awards, an Academy Award, and even a Presidential Medal of Freedom. His remarkable collection of hits over the past sixty years has shaped the music industry and includes such masterpieces as "Like a Rolling Stone" (1965), "Just Like a Woman" (1966), and "Tangled Up In Blue" (1975).

Dylan is known to enjoy his drink and various tipples

feature prominently in many of his lyrics. Perhaps most tellingly, Dylan is an owner of whiskey company Heaven's Door. About this, he's said: "I wanted to create a collection of American whiskeys that, in their own way, tell a story. I've been traveling for decades, and I've been able to try some of the best whiskey spirits that the world has to offer. This is great whiskey."[55] When asked about Dylan's contributions to the company, master blender Ryan Perry shared: "We brought the whiskey expertise, and he brought the creativity. . . . He'd say, 'I want it to taste more like a wooden structure.' I've never had that kind of feedback."[56] We're not sure what that means, but if it's led to a well-balanced bourbon, then please sign us up.

1 ½ ounces Heaven's Door
Straight Bourbon

Pour bourbon into a tulip-shaped copita-style glass. Sip slowly to enjoy, making sure to remember the direction home.

1941

Neil Diamond's
LOVE ON THE ROCKS

🍸 ⚡ SERVES 1

Singer-songwriter and all-around good guy Neil Diamond has been performing since 1962 and has sold nearly 100 million albums. Diamond's multiple chart-topping hits include such classics as "Sweet Caroline" (1969), "Cracklin' Rosie" (1980), and "Love on the Rocks" (1980).

While Diamond has a hit song, "Red Wine" (1967), devoted to praising red wine, we have reason to believe his drink of choice would really be this Love on the Rocks cocktail. In an "Ask Me Anything" forum on Reddit, when one user asked, "If Love on the Rocks was a cocktail, what would it be?," Diamond responded by sharing: "Probably U-Bet chocolate syrup. I love it. Mix some milk in there, put some seltzer in there, mix it up, and you got the greatest, most refreshing drink you'll ever have. An egg cream cocktail is what I would end up with. It's a New York concoction and everybody in the city knows what it is."[57] The recipe the Brooklyn-born star shared would serve up a perfect egg cream for kids and adults of all ages. For those of us over twenty-one, feel free to enjoy this version with a little bourbon for good measure.

| 2 tablespoons Fox's U-Bet chocolate syrup | 1 ½ ounces whole milk | ¾ cup seltzer water ½ ounce bourbon (optional) |

Combine all ingredients in a chilled cocktail shaker, then pour into a coupe glass. Enjoy with Diamond's song of the same name setting the mood. Share with a loved one and don't require anyone to be accountable for what they share while sipping the sweet concoction.

Remember, *"Love on the rocks, ain't no big surprise. Just pour me a drink and I'll tell you my lies. . . ."*

1942

Carole King's
CHAMPAGNE COCKTAIL

SERVES 1

L egendary songwriter Carole King wrote or cowrote such
rock standards as "The Loco-Motion" (1962), "One Fine
Day" (1964), and "(You Make Me Feel Like) A Natural Woman"
(1967), and found success as a solo performer with the 1971
album *Tapestry*, which would sell twenty-five million albums
and chart for six years in the US. She would later prove to be
one of the most successful female songwriters, penning 118
songs that hit the Billboard Hot 100 list.

But while King made a name for herself in the music
world, she did not fall victim to the drug and alcohol abuse so

prevalent within the industry. Her memoir, *A Natural Woman*, is an account of hard work, drinking in moderation, abstaining from drugs, and devoting herself to getting a solid eight hours of sleep per night. She does, however, share one scene of drinking champagne in a friend's apartment—and the classy elixir features prominently in the song "Tonight You're All Mine" (2004), which she shared with Ann Hampton Callaway, with the lyrics advising a lover to "Light up some candles, chill some champagne, draw us a bath, baby, [and] put on Coltrane."

Given King's taste for champagne, we think she'd enjoy this champagne cocktail. A staunch environmentalist, she'd certainly use sugar from an eco-friendly manufacturer and organic fruit for the garnish. Channel her by doing the same.

1 cube natural sugar	2 dashes bitters
6 ounces brut champagne, chilled	Organic lemon twist for garnishing

Drop the sugar cube and bitters into a champagne flute, fill the glass with champagne, and garnish with the lemon twist. Enjoy while blasting "A Natural Woman" or gather your besties and sip while swaying softly to "You've Got a Friend" (1971).

1942

Paul McCartney's
CLEMENTINE MACCARITA

SERVES 1

S ir Paul McCartney penned some of rock's most beloved hits as a member of the Beatles, and has had a successful career since the band's breakup as well. Among the most memorable songs he wrote or cowrote as a Beatle are "And I Love Her" (1964) and "Yesterday" (1965). Hits from his career after include "Band on the Run" (1973) and "Uncle Albert/Admiral Halsey" (1971), the latter the result of a collaboration between McCartney and his wife, Linda.

McCartney is an animal-rights activist who embraces a vegetarian diet, and he doesn't drink before performing (lest he forget the song lyrics), but he does like to let loose and enjoy a good margarita. Confirmation of this comes from a private pilot who once shared, "I've flown McCartney a few times. ... He always has this same margarita in his rider as a standard request,"[58] as well as McCartney's daughter Mary, host of *Mary McCartney Serves It Up!*, who was given the okay to share her dad's recipe for his beloved clementine margarita on her program. Reportedly McCartney likes to call it a "maccarita."[59] As Mary shared, "It's a margarita but it's his version. It's got a couple of secret ingredients in it."[60]

1 lime, halved	¾ ounce Cointreau liqueur	Juice of 1 clementine, freshly squeezed
Fine sea salt, to taste		
2 ¼ ounces good-quality blanco tequila	¾ ounce triple sec	

Rub the rim of a margarita glass with 1 lime half to moisten, then coat the rim with sea salt. Pour the tequila, Cointreau, triple sec, and clementine juice into a cocktail shaker and squeeze in the juice of the remaining lime half. Add ice and shake vigorously. Strain into the prepared margarita glass.

1943

Joni Mitchell's
LEMON SAKE

SERVES 1

The great Joni Mitchell has been described by *Rolling Stone* as a "genius singer-songwriter . . . [whose] songcraft and recordings have remained essential maps, blueprints, and touchstones, setting standards by which we measure how deep a song can go emotionally, or how much musical invention it can contain."[61] Her musical career began in her native Canada and she moved to Southern California in her twenties, where she would soon find her tunes embracing folk, jazz, rock, and pop. Today, she is a music icon whose songs helped define the counterculture movement of the sixties and seventies and who is the recipient of nine Grammy Awards. Among her hits are such heartwarming classics as "Big Yellow Taxi" (1970), "A Case of You" (1971), and "Both Sides, Now," which she first released in 1969 and released a new version of in 2000.

Although the trailblazing artist is known for being fiercely private and has not publicly shared her preferred brew, a *Washington Post* article on backstage rider requirements reveals that one of Mitchell's riders required sake, and we can certainly imagine the singer kicking back with a glass of the grain alcohol.[62] For a "big yellow" twist, go for this lemon version.

3 ounces dry sake	1 ounce simple syrup	Lemon twist for garnishing
1 ounce lemon juice, freshly squeezed		

Combine the sake, lemon juice, and simple syrup in an ice-filled cocktail shaker. Shake, strain into a martini glass, and garnish with the lemon twist. Enjoy while painting, playing the guitar, writing poetry, or philosophizing.

1943

Keith Richards's
NUCLEAR WASTE

SERVES 1

Considered one of the greatest guitarists of all time, Keith Richards cofounded the Rolling Stones with Mick Jagger and has been a quintessential rock star since 1960. The Stones were inducted into the Rock and Roll Hall of Fame in 1989, have sold more than 240 albums, and were ranked the second greatest artists of all time (behind the Beatles) by *Rolling Stone*. Among Richards's top songs with the band are "You Got the Silver" (1969), "Happy" (1972), and "Before They Make Me Run" (1978).

An intense, highly talented artist who has been known to indulge, Richards's drink of choice is believed to be a vodka and orange soda concoction known as a nuclear waste. In one interview he shared, "I don't know how I fell upon it.... I think it really just happened that one day I had some vodka and nothing to mix it with, so I flung and said well, yeah, I can hang with this."[63] His appreciation for the drink was further documented by a reporter who noted that during their interview, Richards was "drinking a 'nuclear waste'—two ounces of vodka, orange soda, and lots of ice—which his assistant makes throughout the course of the night using small airplane Absolut bottles stored in a cardboard box."[64] To channel the singer then, go for this brew, and note that the coincidence that Jagger and Richards both like an orange beverage mixed with alcohol as their drink of choice is not lost on us either.

2 ounces vodka
1 ounce
orange soda

Orange slice
for garnishing

Mix vodka and soda in an ice-filled cocktail shaker until well combined, then strain into a collins glass filled with ice. Garnish with the orange slice. Enjoy before they make you run.

1943

Mick Jagger's
TEQUILA SUNRISE

SERVES 1

One of the most famous rock stars of all time, singer, songwriter, and hard rocking party boy Sir Michael "Mick" Jagger was a cofounder of the Rolling Stones. Among Jagger and the Stones' most memorable hits are "(I Can't Get No) Satisfaction" (1965), "Sympathy for the Devil" (1968), and "Gimme Shelter" (1969). The songs were groundbreaking, and their musicians eccentric. In one interview, Jagger reflected on the peak years of his career, noting: "I wasn't *trying* to be rebellious in those days. I was just being me."[65]

It's been said that Jagger could be very strict with his routine—sometimes not drinking at all while on the road so as to be properly prepared for his performances—but he was also known to on other occasions let the libations flow freely.[66] Jagger's favorite drink is believed to be a tequila sunrise, and legend has it that Jagger was served his first of these cocktails during a private party for the Stones' 1972 tour. At the time, he'd requested a margarita but the bartender encouraged him to give a tequila sunrise a try. Reportedly, Jagger and the Stones loved the concoction so much that the band ended up ordering them at bars throughout the US during their cross-country tour, which would be dubbed the "cocaine and tequila sunrise tour" in Keith Richards's autobiography.[67] With their endorsement, the drink's popularity soared so much that Jose Cuervo began putting a recipe for tequila sunrise on its tequila bottles.

1 ounce Jose Cuervo Especial Silver tequila

2 ounces orange juice, freshly squeezed

1 teaspoon grenadine

Orange wedge for garnishing

Maraschino cherry for garnishing

Pour tequila and orange juice into a collins glass filled with ice. Slowly add in grenadine and mix, then add the garnishes. Enjoy as you see if the drink brings that long-coveted satisfaction. We know you try, and you try. . . .

Roger Waters's
DARK SIDE OF THE MOON BEER COCKTAIL

SERVES 1

The brilliant singer, songwriter, and bassist Roger Waters cofounded the band that would become Pink Floyd with Syd Barrett, Rick Wright, and Bob Klose in 1965. The band would become the face of progressive rock, producing such hits as "Time" (1973), part of the brilliant *Dark Side of the Moon* album, "Wish You Were Here" (1975), and "Comfortably Numb" (1975), and would sell more than 250 million albums. But while the band's psychedelic, philosophical lyrics were acquiring legions of fans worldwide, they had their struggles. Barrett's use of psychedelic drugs and mental health issues led to him being ousted from the band in 1968, at which time Waters became the mastermind behind most of their new lyrics and the band's image. But the band would crumble under tension and Waters would depart in 1985 to embark on a solo career.

While Pink Floyd's music is often associated with hallucinogens and Barrett's struggles have been well-publicized, Waters was not known for overindulging—although he did have a period when he mixed nicotine and hashish into joints he'd smoke throughout the day.[68] As for alcohol, his go-to is believed to be nothing more than a simple ale. With that in mind, those looking to channel him might do best by kicking back with this *Dark Side of the Moon*–inspired beer cocktail.

6 ounces
Blue Moon beer

6 ounces
Guinness Extra Stout

Lime
wedge for
garnishing

Fill a pint glass half full with the Blue Moon and top with the Guinness. Stir well and garnish with the lime wedge. Stop drinking if you have become comfortably numb.

1944

Diana Ross's
COFFEE WITH COGNAC

SERVES 1

The lead singer for the Supremes and later a successful solo artist, Diana Ross has been performing for more than six decades. Ross's music career began in her teen years as a member of the Primettes, and the band would later be picked up by Motown Records on the condition that they change their name to the Supremes. After Ross was assigned the role of lead singer, the band's name was changed to Diana Ross and the Supremes. The band would become one of Motown's most successful music groups and one of the best-selling female groups of all time, with twelve of their songs reaching the top spot on the Billboard Hot 100 list. In 1968, Ross would begin performing as a solo artist. To date she has been inducted into the Rock and Roll Hall of Fame, been recognized by *The Guinness Book of World Records* for having more hit songs than any other female artist in the US or UK, received a Grammy Lifetime Achievement Award, and received a Presidential Medal of Freedom. Among her hits are "Ain't No Mountain High Enough" (1970), a cover that Ross transformed into her own, "I'm Coming Out" (1980), and "Endless Love" (1981), a duet between Ross and Lionel Richie, which Billboard has named the greatest duet of all time.

The legendary Ross has been known to indulge with the occasional cocktail and reportedly is especially partial to vodka, brandy, and cognac. One reporter noted Ross's order of a vodka gimlet and another noted that at a recording session she requested a "small snifter of T. Hines & Co. cognac."[69] [70] According to biographer J. Randy Taraborrelli, Ross "would definitely have a few snifters of brandy when recording" and "liked a little cognac in her coffee right before walking onto a stage."[71] That said, Ross has been to rehab for drug and alcohol use, so make sure to indulge in moderation. We love the idea of one coffee with cognac before going on whatever the stage in your life is.

| 8 ounces brewed coffee | 1 ½ ounces cognac | Splash milk of choice (optional) |

Mix cognac into a mug filled with coffee and add milk of choice. Drink while singing along to Ross's biggest hits and letting the world know that you're coming out.

1944

Jimmy Page's
SWIG OF JACK

SERVES 1

Jimmy Page is considered one of the great guitarists of all time. His career began in England in the mid-1960s, and he formed Led Zeppelin with Robert Plant, John Bonham, and John Paul Jones in 1968. The band would quickly become a face of rock and roll—with wild onstage jam sessions bursting with energy and its members the indulgent party boys of rock.

Today Led Zeppelin has sold more than 300 million albums, received a lifetime achievement award, and have such hits to their name as "Whole Lotta Love" (1969), "Stairway to Heaven" (1971), and "Black Dog" (1971). The band broke up in 1980 following Bonham's death, which was believed to be tied to his alcohol consumption, and in recent years Page has said he no longer drinks alcohol. But a look back at photos from the heyday of Zeppelin brings up numerous images of Page chugging straight from a bottle of Jack. It's even been said that Page "helped make Jack Daniel's the swig of choice for rock rebels."[72] With that in mind, channel the rock star by a simple swig straight from the bottle.

══

750-milliliter bottle Jack Daniel's
Old No. 7 whiskey

══

Take a swig of Jack straight from the bottle and then let it rip on the guitar, unleashing your most epic riffs.

Carly Simon's
CHÂTEAUNEUF-DU-PAPE

SERVES 1

The great singer-songwriter Carly Simon is known for her talent and charm. She is the daughter of a civil rights activist mother and her father was the cofounder of the publishing house Simon & Schuster, so Simon grew up surrounded by activists and literary icons. In 1964 she began performing with her sister in a band aptly named the Simon Sisters, and later embarked on a solo career. Her hits have included such classics as "You're So Vain" (1972)—which would receive endless speculation as to which of Simon's famous lovers was the subject, actor Warren Beatty being a top contender—"Legend in Your Own Time" (1972), and "Coming Around Again" (1986). Simon has received two Grammy Awards, an Academy Award, and a Golden Globe.

But Simon's path to success was not easy; her father died when Simon was a teenager and Simon has overcome challenges including a stammer, a failed first marriage due to her husband's drug and alcohol abuse, and a failed second marriage due to her husband's closeted sexuality.

In Simon's memoir she writes of spending time during her college years in France's Châteauneuf-du-Pape region with a boyfriend. Simon would cook regularly and every night the couple "washed down . . . dinner and dessert with a shared bottle of local wine, almost always a Châteauneuf-du-Pape."[73] To channel Simon, we suggest treating yourself to a bottle of this delicious French grenache-based red wine blend. Unfortunately in a later period, after trying the wine in New York, Simon would realize she has an allergy to the wine that was responsible for what she took to be a nervous breakdown in France—so if you, too, are allergic, it's best to stay clear! If not, indulge freely. Consider pairing with a slice of brandied fruitcake, as Simon writes in her memoir that during her days of drinking Châteauneuf-du-Pape, she was often baking desserts filled with dried fruits, pine nuts, brandy, and wine—and a brandied fruitcake should achieve the same taste bud–delighting effect.

5 ounces Châteauneuf-du-Pape red wine	1 slice brandied fruitcake for pairing (optional)

Pour wine into a red wine glass and sip between bites of the fruitcake. Best enjoyed with the knowledge that you are a legend in your own time and taking digs at unnamed ex-lovers through song is almost always a good idea.

1945

Debbie Harry's
WHITE WINE SPRITZER

SERVES 1

The iconic Debbie Harry was the lead singer for Blondie and has had a successful solo career as well, in addition to major acting roles. Together with guitarist Chris Stein (Harry's partner for many years), Harry cofounded the punk-edged new wave rock band Blondie, which produced such hits as "Heart of Glass"(1978), "One Way or Another" (1978), and "Rapture" (1980), which was the first rap song to chart at number one in the US.

Harry's and Stein's youth saw an indulgence in drugs followed by rehab, and today Harry is very health conscious. She is, however, partial to a glass of Chardonnay, and once recalled, "I was at a festival in Europe—I can't remember where—and the promoter was really into wine. He brought out of a bottle of Chardonnay that I probably would have slept with if it had been a person."[74] She especially favors the Chardonnays produced by Cakebread Cellars.[75] Her perfect accompaniment? Dark chocolate.

4 ounces Cakebread Cellars Chardonnay, very cold

1 ounce club soda, very cold

Lime slice for garnishing

Dark chocolate for pairing (optional)

Fill a white wine glass most of the way with ice. Add the cold Chardonnay and club soda and stir. Garnish with the lime slice. If one way or another, you're gonna channel Harry, pair the spritzer with a side of dark chocolate. Then she'll get ya, she'll get ya . . . .

Cakebread Cellars

Chardonnay

NAPA VALLEY

1945

Eric Clapton's
VODKA LAGER

SERVES 1

"To be on stage, you were almost expected to be drunk. I remember doing one entire show lying down on the stage with the microphone stand lying beside me, and nobody batted an eyelid . . . probably because the audience was as drunk as I was." —Eric Clapton

The legendary rock icon Eric Clapton is widely regarded as one of the best guitarists of all time, in addition to being a talented singer-songwriter. He received his first guitar at age thirteen and would go on to play with bands such as Cream before embarking on a solo career in 1970. Among Clapton's hits are "Layla" (1971), his cover of Bob Marley's "I Shot the Sheriff" (1974), and "Wonderful Tonight" (1977). In his solo career he has sold more than 280 million albums, and he has received eighteen Grammy Awards.

But while Clapton is a music pro and delights audiences, he has had setbacks, including at least one drunken onstage rant. Today he is sober, but for years he was a heavy drug user and binge drinker. In his memoir, he shares, "brandy was my drink of choice, but I couldn't drink it neat. Like most alcoholics I have met since, I didn't like the taste of alcohol, so I would mix with something sweet, like ginger ale or 7-Up."[76] In interviews, he has also shared how he had a taste for a mixed drink of Carlsberg Special Brew lager with vodka. In speaking with BBC Radio 2, he revealed: "For at least twenty years I was a basket case, and that is putting it lightly. I drank more than you can imagine, a Special Brew with vodka."[77] To channel Clapton in his wilder years enjoy that brew yourself, but remember, easy does it. If you're looking to channel the sober Clapton, go straight to the sweet stuff with a ginger ale or 7-Up and turn the volume up high.

320-milliliter can Carlsberg
Special Brew lager

¾ ounce
vodka

Stir beer and vodka together in a pint glass. Let yourself feel
wonderful tonight.

1945

John Fogerty's
LAGERITA

SERVES 1

L ead singer, songwriter, and guitarist for Creedence
Clearwater Revival (CCR) in addition to having a successful
solo career, John Fogerty is a legend in the American rock
scene. Fogerty's interest in the music world began early; he was
only in middle school when he formed the band that would
transition through multiple names before becoming Creedence
Clearwater Revival in 1968. Fogerty would play in CCR through
1972, when the band split, and then embark on a solo career.
Among his hit songs are "Fortunate Son" (1969), "Proud Mary"
(1969), and "The Old Man Down the Road" (1984).

It's believed that today Fogerty rarely drinks, but he has
shared how he drank heavily for many years and the subject

was covered in his memoir. In one scene in the memoir, his wife, Julie Kramer, shared her first experience meeting Fogerty, noting: "John was a little rough around the edges. . . . He kept ordering straight shots of tequila and chasing them with a beer."[78] To channel Fogerty in his drinking days feel free to go that route, but if that's too rough for you, try the classic beer and tequila cocktail: the lagerita.

2 ounces tequila	1 ounce lime juice,	1 lime wedge
¾ ounce	freshly squeezed	for garnishing
Cointreau liqueur	4 ounces lager	

Combine all ingredients except garnish in a cocktail shaker. Pour into a tulip glass and garnish with the lime wedge.

TIP: When Fogerty first met Kramer and asked to buy her a drink, she requested a Peachtree on the rocks, much to his surprise and confusion. This refreshing brew is simply peach schnapps liqueur on ice and we highly recommend it if a Lagerita simply ain't you.

1945

Pete Townshend's
RÉMY OLD-FASHIONED

SERVES 1

Pete Townshend was cofounder of the Who, and for the past sixty years has delighted audiences as a guitarist and singer-songwriter for the band and as a solo artist. His impressive record includes having composed much of the Who's rock opera album *Tommy* (1969) and all of its album *Quadrophenia* (1973).

Today Townshend is sober, but he is open about how alcohol and drugs were frequently used by members of the Who during its heyday. "Alcohol was valuable because it loosened me up creatively," he has said, along with admitting that he used to drink Rémy Martin cognac by the pint.[79] On the inner sleeve of his album *Empty Glass* (1980), he even thanked Rémy Martin, with the comment: "Thanks to Rémy Martin cognac for saving my life by making the bloody stuff so expensive"—perhaps a recognition that he could have overindulged, and the price point was what prevented the drinking from worsening. In his memoir, Townshend shared: "My capacity for booze while on stage was enormous, especially if I stuck to cognac."[80] He has also revealed that for fifteen years he was sustained by cognac, saying, "I didn't drink any water, I didn't drink any tea, I didn't drink Coca-Cola. I don't think I ate. I just lived on cognac."[81]

While Townshend took his Rémy straight, he would certainly have enjoyed this old-fashioned with it. If you're summoning the legend during the Who's defining years, enjoy the traditional cocktail. To channel Townshend today, go for a mocktail by swapping the cognac for cold-brewed barley tea.

½ teaspoon sugar

3 dashes angostura bitters

2 ounces Rémy Martin VSOP cognac or cold-brewed barley tea

Orange peel for garnishing

Combine sugar, bitters, and 1 teaspoon water in a rocks glass and stir to dissolve the sugar. Fill the glass with ice and add cognac. Garnish with the orange peel.

1945

Ritchie Blackmore's
PURPLE WHISKEY

SERVES 1

The hard rock and heavy metal performer Ritchie Blackmore is considered one of the greatest and most influential guitarists. A cofounder of Deep Purple, Blackmore has also had a successful solo career and established the band Rainbow. Among the hits Blackmore has written or cowritten are "Smoke on the Water" (1972), "Burn" (1974), and "Stargazer" (1976).

Blackmore has described his image as dark and moody[82] and he has been known to lash out or act outrageously; once hurling a steak and baked potato across a high-end restaurant because he felt the potato was overcooked; another time, after being called onstage earlier than he'd wanted, having his amps doused in gasoline, which caused them to explode and blow a hole in the stage. The damage resulted in the need to evacuate the venue and pay a ten-thousand-dollar repair fee.

Blackmore's over-the-top behavior likely stems from the combination of a naturally wild personality with drinking, which he's never shied away from speaking about. He's shared events following vodka consumption—such as asking Deep Purple's Ian Gillian to join Rainbow and then regretting the request—and his love of malt whiskey, particularly Johnnie Walker Black Label, is well-known.[83] Blackmore reportedly even marks his bottles so he knows how much he can safely drink before a show—and once lowered the line after a falling out with Rainbow's Graham Bonnet.[84]

While Blackmore, often called "the man in black," would drink whiskey straight from his marked bottle, try this refined cocktail for a Deep Purple twist. Enjoy against a hard rock soundtrack with a monster riff.

1 cup blueberries
(reserve some for garnishing)

1 ounce blueberry schnapps

1 ½ ounces Johnnie Walker
Black Label Scotch whisky

Splash grape juice

Muddle together blueberries
and schnapps, then add the
whisky. Pour into a collins
glass and add ice and a splash
of grape juice. Garnish with
reserved blueberries. Enjoy
while dressed in black and
raging heavily.

1945

Rod Stewart's
RUM AND COKE

SERVES 1

S ir Rod Stewart, the legendary rocker behind such mega hits
as "Maggie May" (1971), "Hot Legs" (1977), and "Da Ya Think
I'm Sexy?" (1978) has been performing for more than sixty years.
With his unique raspy voice, Stewart has sung disco, new wave,
pop, and rock, performing with the Jeff Beck Group, the Faces,
and ultimately as a solo artist. With his bandmates in the Faces,
drinking and carousing were pretty much a way of life.

"We were outrageous with the Faces," Stewart told *The
Late Late Show*'s James Corden when he appeared on "Carpool
Karaoke." "Just drinking and shagging and a-drinking and

a-shagging, basically that's what we did, and smashing up hotel rooms." Because of their behavior, the band was eventually banned from all Holiday Inns.

Today Stewart says he enjoys two glasses of white wine and a glass of red wine and then sleeps "very, very well."[85] But as he wrote in his biography, he used to go harder: "The Faces were prodigious drinkers. Drink gave you the necessary courage to go slightly under-rehearsed into the night. Spirits and wine were especially helpful in this regard. . . Recording sessions with The Faces always started out in the pub. . . . You believed that nothing would get the recording process flowing like a round of rum and Cokes—except possibly another round of rum and Cokes."[86]

Stewart's song "The Drinking Song" (2015) chronicles his mostly true inebriated exploits over the years. When you enjoy a rum and Coke and settle in to get your creative juices flowing, take heed of the song's lyrics: "If ya take to the drinking, you're gonna make mistakes." Know, though, that Stewart says despite the antics his drinking inspired, he wouldn't change a thing.

2 ounces rum

4 ounces Coca-Cola

Lime wedge for garnishing

Fill a highball glass with ice
and add the rum. Top with
Coca-Cola and stir. Garnish
with the lime wedge.

Cher's
STRAWBERRY
DAIQUIRI

SERVES 1

Cher is another member of rock's royal family and one of the most successful ladies of rock. Her career, which has spanned six decades and counting, first took off after she met Sonny Bono at age sixteen and the couple formed the band Sonny and Cher. The duo would produce such hits as "Baby Don't Go" (1964), "I Got You Babe" (1965), and "The Beat Goes On" (1967). After their split, Cher would have an epic solo career with hits including "Take Me Home" (1979), "If I Could Turn Back Time" (1989), and "Believe" (1998), and in her solo career she has sold more than 100 million albums.

A solid rock goddess all around, Cher is known for her philanthropic and advocacy work in addition to her music, dramatic roles, and unique style. The diet that keeps her going is known to be plant-based and she limits her alcohol consumption. Still, she will treat herself on occasion. On a night out with friends in Italy, for example, she was photographed enjoying a strawberry daiquiri.[87] And the occasional daiquiri is certainly something we can get behind. To channel Cher, allow yourself the occasional sweet indulgence as well.

¼ pound ripe strawberries (reserve some for garnishing)

1 ¼ tablespoons simple syrup

1 tablespoon lime juice, freshly squeezed

2 ounces light rum (optional)

Dash salt

Combine all ingredients except garnish with ice in a blender and blend until smooth. Pour into a martini glass and garnish with strawberries. Best enjoyed while donning a feather headdress and a long, glittery gown, dancing freely, and believing in life after love.

1946

Jimmy Buffett's
MARGARITA

SERVES 1

Singer-songwriter Jimmy Buffett has delighted fans with his country rock music and laid-back, beach-vibes persona for nearly sixty years. His global hit "Margaritaville" (1977) was inducted into the Grammy Hall of Fame for its cultural and historic significance, and its release was followed by the popular song "Cheeseburger in Paradise" (1978). In later years, Buffett and Alan Jackson created the hit "It's Five O'Clock Somewhere" (2003). Crowds of "Parrot Heads," Buffett devotees, are fans of the singer and embrace the laid-back lifestyle he sings about.

With Buffett's early hits, he built a brand that included a worldwide chain of Margaritaville and Cheeseburger in Paradise–themed restaurants and hotels, as well as a signature Margaritaville tequila, Landshark beer, a Broadway musical, and more. But while Buffett owns many food and drink establishments, the singer says he no longer consumes sugar or carbs, except on Sundays, and is more partial to tequila on the rocks, only occasionally enjoying a margarita.[88] While we are fans of this classic margarita recipe he has shared, if you prefer to channel the singer today, replace with tequila on the rocks.[89] Enjoy either drink any time it's five o'clock somewhere.

Salt to rim the glass (optional)	¼ ounce Margaritaville Tequila Silver	¼ ounce orange curaçao
½ ounce Margaritaville Tequila Gold	¼ ounce triple sec	¼ ounce lime juice, freshly squeezed
		2 lime wedges

Rim a margarita glass with salt and set aside. Combine all other ingredients except lime wedges in a cocktail shaker filled with ice. Squeeze in the juice of 1 lime wedge, then drop both wedges in. Cover, shake vigorously, and strain into the prepared margarita glass. For good measure, enjoy while nibbling on sponge cake and watchin' the sun bake.

1946

Linda Ronstadt's
HORCHATA

SERVES 6

A defining female voice in rock history, Linda Ronstadt fused elements of rock, folk, country, Latin, and pop to create her velvety tunes. She began playing music in her youth with her brother and sister, but really made a name for herself in California in the mid-1960s after cofounding the band the Stone Poneys. The band would play together for three years before Ronstadt embarked on a solo career. By the late 1970s, she had six platinum-certified albums, three of which charted in the top position on the Billboard list, and was the highest-paid woman in rock. Today, Ronstadt has produced twenty-four studio albums and won eleven Grammy Awards.

Her hit songs include "Long, Long Time" (1970), "You're No Good" (1974), a cover of a song by Dee Dee Warwick that Ronstadt made a chart-topping hit, and "Desperado" (1975), a dazzling cover of the Eagles' song.

Ronstadt was born in Arizona and her father is of partial Mexican descent, which has influenced her food and drink preferences, although she does not drink alcohol due to an allergy. In her memoir she shares, "I attempted to get drunk a few times by drinking tequila, my father's drink of choice. The result was a bright red face and several days of throwing up."[90] This means no margarita for Ronstadt, but we know she has a taste for burritos and other Mexican dishes, and we think she'd agree that a horchata is a delightful way to channel her.[91] The horchata is a classic Mexican drink made from rice, vanilla, and cinnamon.

1 cup uncooked
long-grain
white rice

8 cinnamon sticks
(reserve 6 for
garnishing)

1 ½ cups milk
of choice

2 teaspoons
vanilla extract

½ cup
granulated sugar

2 teaspoons
ground
cinnamon

Blend rice, 2 cinnamon sticks, and 4 cups water in a blender, then pour into a pitcher with a tight lid and let rest at room temperature for at least 8 hours. Strain and discard the rice, then stir in all remaining ingredients. Serve in ice-filled collins glasses and garnish each glass with a cinnamon stick. Enjoy while shattering glass ceilings and being a master of your craft.

1946

Patti Smith's
AMERICANO

SERVES 1

S inger, songwriter, poet, National Book Award winner, and all-around creative spirit Patti Smith was one of the most powerful female voices defining the burgeoning punk rock scene of the 1970s. Living in New York City in her twenties, Smith began to experiment with turning her poetry into lyrics and soon formed the Patti Smith Group. In 1975, Smith would release the album *Horses*, and the album would kickstart her music career. Among Smith's hit songs to date are "Gloria" (1975), "Because the Night" (1978), which she cowrote with Bruce Springsteen, and "Dancing Barefoot" (1979).

While Smith has been known to enjoy marijuana, she's not known to drink much alcohol. What she does enjoy repeatedly, she has shared, is coffee, particularly an Americano.[92] Coffee features prominently in her memoir *M Train*, and a lovely review in the *New Yorker* describes how coffee "courses through her memoir . . . like a dark, steaming river, connecting her various adventures . . . . but she's no snob: a large serving from 7-Eleven—accompanied, on occasion, by a glazed doughnut—will do, if necessary."[93]

To channel Smith, go for her favorite beverage. Skip the 7-Eleven junk and have a hearty home-brewed Americano. If this doesn't unleash your creative juices, try adding a splash of Kahlúa and go for the glazed doughnut as well.

2 ounces espresso

1 ounce Kahlúa (optional)

Glazed doughnut
for pairing (optional)

Brew the espresso in an espresso maker, then add 4 ounces hot water, stir, and pour into a coffee mug. Add the Kahlúa and pair with the doughnut. Make sure to have a journal nearby and let the poetry flow between sips. If you find the words come out in song, all the better. Dance barefoot once caffeinated.

1947

Don Henley's
SCOTINI

Hotel California

🥃 ⚡ **SERVES 1**

S inger, songwriter, drummer, guitarist, and cofounder of
the Eagles Don Henley was instrumental in many of the
band's hit songs, and has had a successful solo career as well.
Henley would meet Glenn Frey in 1971 and together with Randy
Meisner and Bernie Leadon form the Eagles that same year.
Henley and his bandmates infused Eagles songs with a unique
blend of rock, country, folk, and pop music, and the band
would sell more than 150 million albums and win six Grammy
Awards. The Eagles would break up in 1980 but reunite in 1994,
with Henley embracing his solo career in the interim years.
Among Henley's biggest hits are "Hotel California" (1976), "The
Last Resort" (1976), and "Boys of Summer" (1984).

Today Henley drinks very little alcohol. He has shared that "There's no partying, no alcohol, it's like a morgue backstage" and when he does indulge it tends to be "a good glass of claret" wine with dinner at his Texas ranch home.[94][95] But during the heyday of the Eagles, the band members were known for their enjoyment of all kinds of brews (and cocaine). In Marc Eliot's book *To the Limit: The Untold Story of The Eagles,* Henley recounts how he and Danny "Kootch" Kortchmar liked to drink while they worked, writing: "Kootch and I were just guzzling Scotch and vodka; we'd record until three in the morning and then go to my house, sit up with bottles, and tell each other how great we are."[96] To channel Henley today, keep it classy with a glass of claret at dinner. To channel Henley from his more raucous years, go for a scotini, which brings a little cocktail sophistication to a 3 a.m. Scotch and vodka.

½ cup high-quality vodka   1 tablespoon Scotch whisky

Fill a rocks glass with ice. Add vodka, top with Scotch, and stir. Sip while letting Henley's smooth tunes fill the room and imagining yourself in the Hotel California. *"Such a lovely place."*

1947

Elton John's

JOHNNIE AND LEMON

SERVES 1

Sir Elton John is a five-time Grammy Award–winning singer, pianist, and composer whose breathtaking songs have led to sales of more than 300 million albums. The icon met his musical partner, lyricist Bernie Taupin, in 1967 and together they have produced thirty albums. Among John's remarkable hits are "Your Song" (1970), which was certified double platinum, "Tiny Dancer" (1972), which was also certified double platinum, and "Rocket Man" (1972), which was certified triple platinum.

But while John is known for his smooth tunes, he has faced an uphill battle, at times having to counter anti-LGBTQ prejudices and also having to face his addictions head on. Today John has been sober for more than thirty years, but he has spoken frankly about many years of abusing cocaine and alcohol. In one interview he shared, "Not only was I a drug addict, I was an alcoholic. I used to drink a bottle of Johnnie Walker Black every day."[97] We can't get behind a bottle of whiskey a day, but we can get behind a single solid whiskey cocktail. To channel the legend in his heyday, try this Johnnie Walker Black Label cocktail with lemon to take the edge off.[98] If channeling John in recent years, go for the mocktail tweak.

1 ½ ounces Johnnie Walker Black Label Scotch whisky or freshly squeezed lemon juice

5 ounces carbonated lemonade (such as R.White's Lemonade)

Lemon zest for garnishing

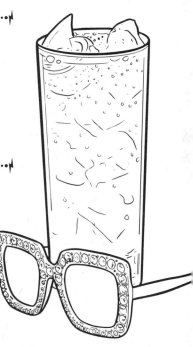

Mix whisky and lemonade together in an ice-filled highball glass, then garnish with the lemon zest. Best enjoyed in a colorful, perfectly tailored suit with large rhinestone-covered, rose-tinted glasses while seated at a piano and smiling coyly at adoring fans.

1947

Ian Anderson's
SCREWDRIVER

SERVES 1

S inger, songwriter, flautist, and guitarist Ian Anderson is the force behind the progressive rock band Jethro Tull, which originated in the late sixties and made the flute an essential part of rock history. The band's song "Aqualung" (1971), with its signature heavy guitar riff, regularly numbers in the top five greatest classic rock songs of all time, and they also produced such chart-topping concept albums as *Thick as a Brick* (1971) and *A Passion Play* (1973).

Jethro Tull's clever and often esoteric lyrics reflect the personality of Anderson, who is artistically minded and a true original. A *Psychology Today* journalist who interviewed

Anderson noted that as his career progressed, the musician began to "make personal and professional decisions that defied conventional norms and standards" and that "while many of his contemporaries were experimenting heavily with drugs and alcohol, he decided to avoid anything that could lead to addiction."[99] To this end, Anderson noted that he has never tried drugs. (He has said, "I don't like anything that changes my perception or my chilling, lizard-like mental capacity."[100]) He does, however, enjoy alcohol in moderation. Today, in his early seventies, he has a "glass of chilled vodka" every morning—though that's where his partaking ends, as he has noted: "I'm one of those people who never drink after mid-morning."[101]

If you share Anderson's lizard-like mental capacity, or aspire to, perhaps you too can take on the day with a glass of chilled vodka providing a jumpstart; our recommendation, however, is to be inspired by Anderson, but enjoy a little OJ with it. Got to have that vitamin C, after all.

| 2 ounces vodka, chilled | 4 ounces orange juice, freshly squeezed | Orange slice for garnishing |

Mix vodka and orange juice in a highball glass with ice and garnish with the orange slice. Enjoy until a lizard-like mental capacity is reached.

TIP: If looking to invoke the Anderson muse after mid-morning, we suggest checking out Anderson's guide to Indian food on the Jethro Tull website.

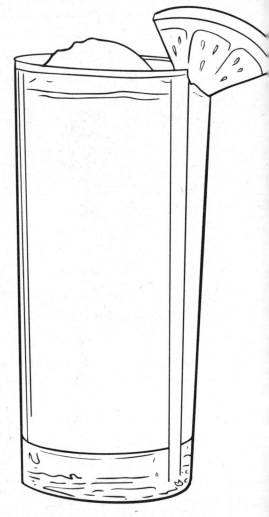

Alice Cooper's
VELVET HAMMER AND TUNA FISH MALTED FOR HANGOVERS

SERVES 1

For nearly sixty years Alice Cooper has been thrilling audiences with his ghoulish and horror-tinged performances. The raspy-voiced singer, who is known as the godfather of shock rock, was a singer-songwriter for the band he took the name Alice Cooper from and has also had a solo career. Among Cooper's notable hits are "I'm Eighteen" (1971), "School's Out" (1972), and "No More Mr. Nice Guy" (1973).

During his rise to fame, Cooper was known for drunken exploits, but that all stopped in 1983 when he was diagnosed with cirrhosis of the liver and his wife filed for divorce, reportedly as a result of Cooper's alcoholism. In response Cooper got sober, and today he continues to rock hard but sans alcohol.

To invoke the macabre Alice Cooper spirit, enjoy this velvet hammer sourced from a wealth of recipes Cooper provided to *Creem* magazine for their 1973 story "Alice Cooper's Alcohol Cookbook and Timetable for World Conquest," which included twenty-two cocktail recipes and one hangover remedy, the tuna fish malted.[102] We know the hangover helper looks like an awful thing to ingest, but hey, being Alice Cooper can't be easy. If you're looking to channel Cooper in more recent years and prefer to avoid getting queasy, we suggest going straight to the pistachio ice cream and reserving the other ingredients for other uses.

VELVET HAMMER

1 ounce gin

1 ounce apricot brandy

1 ounce dry vermouth

Dash maraschino liqueur

Dash orange bitters

Combine all ingredients in an ice-filled cocktail shaker. Strain into a collins glass.

TUNA FISH MALTED FOR HANGOVERS

5-ounce can tuna fish

4 ounces cream

2 scoops pistachio ice cream

Blend all ingredients together and pour into a drinking glass. Drink, and then go back to bed.

1948

Donald Fagen's
PIÑA COLADA

SERVES 1

The beloved rock band Steely Dan was founded in 1972 by singer and keyboardist Donald Fagen and guitarist and bassist Walter Becker. The duo met in college and then moved to New York City, where they refined their style and infused their sound with jazz and other musical styles. For a while they toured, but then chose to focus on their studio recordings, and the result was the creation of such lasting hits as "Reelin' in the Years" (1972), "Rikki Don't Lose That Number" (1974), and "Deacon Blues" (1977).

Although Becker passed away in 2017, Steely Dan's songs continue to enjoy a cult following and are even known to have a devoted fanbase of millennials. As one journalist noted, "Steely Dan, the jazz-rock combo whose musical and lyrical checkpoints include those most boomer-ish of pursuits such as cool jazz, hot guitar licks, tiki drinks, and expensive cocaine, have become an object of millennial obsession, spawning viral tweets, mash-ups, and even a custom run of streetwear emblazoned with their album art."[103]

The reference to tiki drinks surely refers to the frequency with which these drinks appear in the band's song lyrics. In "Haitian Divorce" (1976), an inspired lyric refers to drinking "the zombie from the cocoa shell"; in "Bad Sneakers" (1975), a piña colada is part of the repeating refrain: "Bad sneakers and a piña colada, my friend."

As Steely Dan's lyrics were often up for interpretation, a lot of fans have given great thought to what was being sung about. We suggest making a piña colada, seeing if it connects you to Fagen, and then asking him yourself. If that doesn't work, at least your taste buds will be dancing for joy.

¼ cup diced pineapple, frozen	1 ounce coconut cream	Pineapple slice for garnishing
1 ounce pineapple juice	1 ounce white rum	Maraschino cherry for garnishing
	1 ounce dark rum	

Blend 1 cup ice with frozen pineapple, pineapple juice, coconut cream, and both rums until smooth and frosty. Pour into a poco grande glass and garnish with the pineapple slice and cherry. Wear bad sneakers while enjoying.

1948

Ozzy Osbourne's
BREAKFAST BRANDY
HANGOVER HELPER

SERVES 1

Ozzy Osbourne cofounded Black Sabbath in 1968 and as its lead singer guided the band's rise in the hard rock and heavy metal scene of the 1970s. In 1979 he would be fired from the band as a result of his drug and alcohol abuse, but he would eventually get sober and go on to have a successful career as a solo artist, as well as to star in the reality TV show *The Osbournes*. Among Osbourne's greatest hits are "Black Sabbath" (1970), a song from the band's debut album; "Crazy

Train" (1980), Osbourne's first single as a solo artist; and "Waiting for Darkness" (1983).

Osborne is a larger-than-life personality, and it's known that alcohol and drugs often fueled his "crazy trains." In Osbourne's memoir he shares, "I would drink a bottle of cognac, pass out, wake up, then drink another. I'm not exaggerating when I say I was drinking four bottles of Hennessey a day."[104] Reportedly, Osbourne's addictive behaviors were so extreme that scientists believe his survival must be due to a genetic mutation.[105] Osbourne, however, has shared that he believes his unique hangover cure deserves credit for helping him keep his momentum. In a column for the *Sunday Times Magazine*, he shared: "Over the years, I developed a fail-safe cure. Basically, I'd mix four tablespoons of brandy with four tablespoons of port, throw in some milk, a few egg yolks, and— if I was in a festive mood—some nutmeg. The second I woke, I'd mix it up and down it. The way it works is very clever: it gets you instantly blasted again, so you don't feel a thing."[106] If you're looking to channel the hard rocker in his younger years, give this a go, but proceed with caution unless you share Osbourne's genetic mutation. If you're looking to channel the singer in his more recent years—or are simply feeling drawn to a more reasonable breakfast—skip the brandy and port and enjoy the breakfast on a plate.

2 ounces brandy

2 ounces port wine

Dash milk of choice

2 egg yolks

Sprinkle ground
nutmeg (optional)

Combine all ingredients in a
blender and blend until smooth.
Pour into a collins glass and sip
slowly. Enjoy while donning
round, purple-tinted glasses. Stop
drinking if you begin to feel like
you're aboard a crazy train.

1948

Steven Tyler's
RUSTY NAIL

SERVES 1

Embodying hard rock to his core, Steven Tyler is the lead singer for Aerosmith and one of its founding members, having cofounded the band in 1970. Since then, his long curls, colorful outfits, on-stage acrobatics, and vocals accompanied by wild screams have earned him a reputation and the moniker "the demon of screamin'." To date, the band has received fourteen Grammy Award nominations and four wins. Among Tyler's hits are "Dream On" (1973), "Sweet Emotion" (1975), and "Walk This Way" (1975).

Tyler has spoken openly about his use of alcohol and drugs before getting sober. In the Aerosmith book *Walk This Way*, he recalls that his high school morning routine began at 7:00 a.m. with a plastic juice cup full of Dewar's Scotch.[107] We know this affinity for Scotch lasted because in his memoir, Tyler describes how his favorite cocktail during years of drinking with his bandmates was a rusty nail. He writes, "My favorite cocktail was a rusty nail . . . . Drambuie mixed with the finest Scotch and a twist of lemon." He also shares that he "found out later that Eric Clapton and Ringo Starr were fellow rusty nailers."[108] To channel Tyler in his wild years, definitely go for some Scotch—preferably a rusty nail at happy hour rather than Scotch in a juice cup at seven in the morning. There's unfortunately no way to make a mocktail rusty nail, so to channel the sober Tyler, just head straight for the rock and roll tunes.

1 ½ ounces Scotch whisky	¾ ounce Drambuie liqueur	Lemon zest for garnishing

Mix the Scotch and Drambuie in an ice-filled cocktail shaker until well chilled. Strain into a rocks glass with a large ice cube and garnish with the lemon zest. Sip, sing, and dream on. *"Sing for the laughter, and sing for the tear . . . ."*

1948

Stevie Nicks's
RÉMY SIDECAR

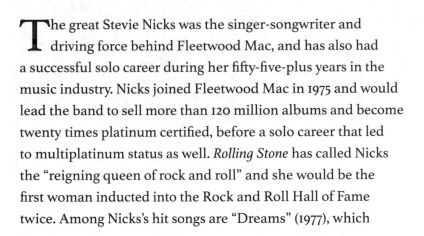

SERVES 1

The great Stevie Nicks was the singer-songwriter and driving force behind Fleetwood Mac, and has also had a successful solo career during her fifty-five-plus years in the music industry. Nicks joined Fleetwood Mac in 1975 and would lead the band to sell more than 120 million albums and become twenty times platinum certified, before a solo career that led to multiplatinum status as well. *Rolling Stone* has called Nicks the "reigning queen of rock and roll" and she would be the first woman inducted into the Rock and Roll Hall of Fame twice. Among Nicks's hit songs are "Dreams" (1977), which would release as a single, sell more than one million copies in the US alone, and reach the top spot on the Billboard Hot 100 list, "Gold Dust Woman" (1977), and "Stop Draggin' My Heart Around" (1981), which she released with Tom Petty and the Heartbreakers and which spent twenty-one weeks on the Billboard list.

Nicks has spoken candidly about the fact that on her rise to the top, she and her bandmates often indulged in drugs and alcohol. Today she is sober, but in reflecting back she has shared how brandy got her through some difficult times, and a peek at one of her backstage riders reveals a preference for Rémy Martin VSOP cognac.[109] [110] To channel Nicks in her Fleetwood Mac years, enjoy a Rémy sidecar. We think Nicks's refined style pairs well with that of the elegant cocktail. To channel her in more recent years, enjoy the mocktail version.

| 2 ounces Rémy Martin VSOP cognac or cold-brew lemon tea | ¾ ounce Cointreau liqueur or freshly squeezed orange juice | ¾ ounce lemon juice, freshly squeezed |
| | | Lemon twist for garnishing |

Mix all ingredients in an ice-filled cocktail shaker. Shake, then strain into a coupe glass and garnish with the lemon twist. Best enjoyed while sporting bell-bottoms, releasing deep, breathy, otherworldly lyrics, and preventing anyone from dragging your heart around.

1949

Billy Gibbons's
THE GIBBONS

SERVES 1

B illy Gibbons, the guitarist and primary singer for ZZ Top, cofounded the band in 1969, and the original lineup's fifty-one years of playing together led them to become the longest-running unchanged lineup in music history, until Dusty Hill's death in 2021. The Houston-based ZZ Top quickly acquired a reputation for its smooth blues-infused rock tunes and the matching look of Gibbons and Hill, who both sported chest-length beards and performed with sunglasses and hats. Among their top hits are "La Grange" (1973), "Tush" (1975), and "Legs" (1983), which would reach number eight on the Billboard Hot 100 list.

As to what brew powers Gibbons, who today has been performing for more than half a century, there are a lot of options. Gibbons is definitely known to indulge in beer drinking, like his bandmates, and reportedly drinks his beers through a straw to "keep the suds from getting in his beard," so beer is one option.[111] Another option is the Crown Royal bourbon earmarked for Gibbons's after-show dressing room on one of ZZ Top's backstage riders.[112] A third option is whatever comprised the massive "chimp in orbit" cocktail that helped Gibbons and his fellow band members get tipsy despite a two-drink minimum in a story he recounted of a performance at a Hawaii venue.[113] Our vote, however, is the gibbons, the tequila drink named after the star, which uses a brand of tequila he pronounced the "best damn tequila you've ever tasted"—even going so far as to invest in the brand and make a promotional video for the cocktail.[114] [115]

1 ½ ounces Pura Vida Reposado tequila	Juice of 1 lemon wedge, freshly squeezed	2 jalapeño slices for garnishing
Juice of 1 lime wedge, freshly squeezed	3 ounces mineral water for topping	

Combine the tequila, lime juice, and lemon juice in an ice-filled cocktail shaker. Strain into an ice-filled highball glass and top with mineral water. Garnish with the jalapeño slices and be sure to drink from a straw so as to keep any facial hair dry. Unleash your best guitar riffs between sips.

Billy Joel's
SODA HIGHBALL

SERVES 1

Singer, songwriter, and pianist Billy Joel has secured twenty-three Grammy nominations and sold more than 150 million albums. His unique rhythmic style has made him one of the most renowned musicians worldwide, and Joel is responsible for such hits as "Piano Man" (1973), which earned him a matching nickname; "New York State of Mind" (1976), which honors the Bronx-born, Long Island-raised New Yorker's hometown; and "Scenes from an Italian Restaurant" (1977).

But while Joel seems utterly composed when performing, he has experienced turbulence in his personal life and has admitted that in past years he occasionally used alcohol to cope. As a result, he mostly sticks to wine today, but for years his preference for Dewar's White Label Scotch was well-known. If you're looking to channel the Piano Man during the peak of his songwriting career, try this classic Dewar's recipe for a soda highball. If you're looking to channel the Piano Man today, have a glass of wine with dinner.

1 ½ ounces Dewar's
White Label Scotch

4 ounces soda water

Lemon twist

Combine Scotch and soda water in a chilled highball glass filled with ice. Twist lemon zest over the drink and garnish with the remainder of the lemon twist. Then sing us a song, like the Piano Man would. *"Yes, sing us a song tonight . . . ."*

1949

Bruce Springsteen and Clarence Clemons's
KAHUNA PUNCH

SERVES 1

Singer-songwriter Bruce Springsteen is a rock legend whose rhythmic tunes have come to define the familiar, comforting music known as heartland rock. To date the New Jersey native has released twenty studio albums, many of them with his E Street Band, and is responsible for such chart-topping hits as "Born to Run" (1975), "Glory Days," (1984), and "Born in the U.S.A." (1984). He has won an astonishing twenty Grammy Awards, an Academy Award, two Golden Globes, a Tony Award, and a Presidential Medal of Freedom, and is a Rock and Roll Hall of Famer.

Springsteen's megastar voice is a sharp departure from his shyness as a child, but he's always been very composed. As he shares in his memoir, his father's alcohol addiction kept Springsteen from trying alcohol until age twenty-two, and he's never been a star known to over-indulge. He does, however, share in his book a scene in which Clarence Clemons, the beloved saxophonist for the E Street Band who was known as the "Big Kahuna," provided the band with "a potent drink mix . . . dubbed 'Kahuna punch.'"[116] What was in that punch we may never know, but as Springsteen has been known to enjoy the occasional tequila shot (which once led to a drunk driving fine), we can imagine that might have been a part of it.

In Springsteen's song "Pink Cadillac" (1985), he belts out: "Now you may think I'm foolish for the foolish things I do"—and we do think that's true when it comes to drinking and driving. So make sure to enjoy this drink safely at home, in a living room infused with the sounds of heartland rock classics.

2 ounces tequila

1 ounce
cranberry juice

1 ounce
grapefruit juice

Splash club soda

Orange slice
for garnishing

Combine tequila, juices, and soda, stirring well. Pour into a collins glass filled with ice and garnish with the orange slice. Drink until you get your fill and don't let a glory day pass you by. Extra points if enjoyed while dancing in the dark.

1949

Gene Simmons's
MILK AND CEREAL
ON THE ROCKS

 SERVES 1

As cofounder, singer, and bassist of the hard rock band Kiss, Gene Simmons has been a force to be reckoned with since he began performing in 1970. Onstage with Kiss he takes on a demon persona, his bandmates take on other personas, and each dons heavy makeup and a spectacular costume, while fire-breathers, shooting guitars, and Simmons's blood-spitting and tongue tricks shock and energize audiences. Among the band's top songs are "Deuce" (1974), "Rock and Roll All Nite" (1975), and "God of Thunder" (1976).

But while Simmons has an otherworldly image, he, unlike

most of his rock peers, has not utilized drugs or alcohol to aid in letting loose. In fact, he has shared, "I literally never drink. Privately or publicly. I simply don't like the taste or the smell of anything with alcohol in it. I have never been drunk in my life and have never taken more than a sip of anything, and hated it every time. I will toast just to be social, but that's it."[117] So what fuels Gene Simmons? Well, we know he's got some pretty unusual tastes—including putting ice cubes into his cereal. In one post to Twitter, his photo shows a mix of Oreo O's cereal and what looks like Frosted Mini Wheats in a bowl with ice. The caption reads, "Anyone else put ice cubes in their cereal?"[118] Our suggestion, then, to invoke the demon is to skip the booze and go straight for cereal on the rocks.

| ½ cup Oreo O's | ½ cup Frosted Mini Wheats | 1 cup milk of choice |

Combine both cereals in a bowl and add milk and ice cubes. Sure, Simmons has a brand of vodka that might also help you channel him, but if he didn't become the wild man he is through booze, then we say go for the cereal with ice and see what happens. Is this the trick to rock and roll all night and party every day?

Ann Wilson's
WHITE LIGHTNING SANGRIA

🍷 ⚡ SERVES 3

Singer-songwriter Ann Wilson and her guitar-playing younger sister, Nancy, are the stars of the band Heart, which is known for its skillful blend of hard rock and folk elements. As the faces of the first female-fronted rock band, the sisters overcame bias and sexism in a male-dominated industry, leading to Heart's rise to fame in the 1970s. Today they've performed for nearly five decades, paved the way for generations of female musicians to follow, sold more than thirty-five million albums, and been inducted into the Rock and Roll Hall of Fame. Wilson has also had a successful solo career, ignited by her dramatic soprano vocal range, operatic additions, and occasional wild banshee screams produced from a powerful voice designed to be heard and to move listeners. Among Wilson's hits are such Heart classics as "Magic Man" (1976), "Crazy on You" (1976), and "Barracuda" (1977), and the band rebooted in the eighties, with MTV regularly playing their power ballads "What About Love" (1985) and "Alone" (1987).

Wilson quit drinking in 2009, noting in her memoir, "Over the years, I built up layers of protection around me, and I often built them up with wine."[119] If you're looking, however, to channel Wilson from Heart's peak years, this white lightning sangria will do the trick. It's inspired by Wilson's penchant for wine and by Heart's song "White Lightning and Wine" (1975)—*"Oh, the world's all mine, white lightning and wine"*—plus a Heart backstage rider's requirement for more than thirteen types of fresh fruit.[120] Or enjoy the mocktail version that Wilson would be more inclined to drink today.

750-milliliter bottle white wine or 1 quart white grape juice, chilled

½ cup vodka (optional)

½ cup sliced grapes

1 green apple, sliced

¼ cup local* strawberries, sliced

¼ cup blueberries, sliced

½ pineapple, sliced

½ cup white sugar (optional; skip if using grape juice instead of wine)

2 cups ginger ale

Combine wine and vodka in a pitcher and stir well. Add sliced fruit, sugar, and ginger ale and stir. Chill, then serve cold in white wine glasses with ice.

* "Local strawberries" were a requirement in the Heart backstage rider, which also noted—in all caps and underlined—that "FRUIT SHOULD NOT BE UNDER OR OVER RIPE." We agree, Ann. No argument there.

1950

Peter Gabriel's
RED RAIN SPRITZER

SERVES 1

The world music champion Peter Gabriel was a founding member of the progressive British rock band Genesis and its lead singer from 1967 to 1975, after which he embarked on a solo career. He would become known worldwide for his unique musical blends, thoughtful lyrics, activism, and founding of the WOMAD arts festivals. Among his hit songs are "Solsbury Hill" (1977), "Sledgehammer" (1986), which reached the number one spot on the Billboard Hot 100 list, and "Red Rain" (1987).

While Gabriel's drink of choice is unknown, it is known that "Red Rain" was inspired by a recurring dream of Gabriel's in which he was swimming in his backyard pool while drinking cold red wine. To channel the star, by all means live out his dream and see what lyrics fill your head—or better yet, simply opt for a cold red wine spritzer.

2 ounces red wine
2 ounces club soda

Fresh mint leaves
for garnishing

Raspberries
for garnishing

Fill a collins glass with ice and stir wine and club soda together in it. Garnish with the mint leaves and raspberries. Sip steadily while writing deep, soulful lyrics with many layers of meaning and pondering how to make the world a better place.

1950

Suzi Quatro's
CHÂTEAU MARGAUX

SERVES 1

D etroit-born singer, songwriter, bass guitarist, and ground-breaking path-paver for women in rock Suzi Quatro rose to fame in the UK before achieving an international following. Her passion for performing took shape in her youth when she first played in her father's jazz band, then formed an all-girl band and was told she would play the bass guitar, which was as large as she was. In 1971 a record producer recruited Quatro to England and helped her embark on a solo career. She would acquire further recognition from a recurring role on *Happy Days*. Today, nearly sixty years after Quatro first began performing, she has sold more than fifty million albums and produced hits including "Can the Can" (1973), which made her the first female bass guitar player to become a major rock star; "Devil Gate Drive (1974); and "Stumblin' In" (1979), a duet with the British singer Chris Norman. Now in her seventies, Quatro continues to perform and can still rock a leather jumpsuit with the best of them.

In Quatro's memoir, she shared, "I *never* drink anything before a show; afterwards, just a glass of wine to make the return journey to the real world a little less traumatic.[121] And although Quatro is not known to be a heavy drinker, she often references her appreciation for wine, particularly red wine. In one interview, in response to what her biggest weakness is, she shared: "Red wine. I'm a bit of a wine snob and like a glass of Châteaux Margaux '82 with a meal or to unwind. But I don't overdo it these days—in my youth I partied with the best of them."[122] To channel the glam rock star, we'll certainly support enjoying a bottle of Château Margaux if you can afford it, but another high-quality red from Bordeaux should do the trick too.

Pour the wine into a red wine glass. Enjoy while partying to channel Quatro in her youth, or sip with a meal if channeling the legend today. For best effects, drink while looking fierce in a tight black leather jumpsuit with a chunky metal belt.

1951

Chrissie Hynde's
TALK OF THE TOWN TEQUILA

SERVES 1

Chrissie Hynde fell in love with rock and roll as a teenager going to concerts, and began playing guitar seriously in her twenties. She longed to be in a band and got her big break when Lemmy Kilmister connected her with the person who would become the first drummer for Hynde's developing band, the Pretenders. The band officially established itself in 1978, with Hynde playing guitar and singing lead vocals. The Pretenders would suffer from the loss of two members to drugs, but Hynde would push forward, leading the group to be inducted into the Rock and Roll Hall of Fame and Hynde to become the leading female voice in new wave rock. Among her hit songs are "Brass in Pocket" (1979), "Talk of the Town" (1981), and "Back on the Chain Gang" (1982).

Today Hynde is sober, but during the formative years of the Pretenders, she was known to indulge. Writing about her youth in her memoir, she shares: "Never mind cocktails, I was happier knocking back straight tequila; it was a lot more to the point, and I've never liked fuss of any kind."[123] And further evidence of her interest in the drink is documented by the Pretenders' aptly named song Tequila (1979) and a Pretenders backstage rider, which includes a requirement for a bottle of Patrón gold tequila (Patrón Añejo).[124] To invoke Hynde in the heyday of the Pretenders, allow yourself a shot of tequila—or go our preferred route with something a tad softer by making our talk of the town tequila concoction, which embraces other requirements of the Pretenders' backstage rider to make a brew similar to a tequila sunrise. We think it still does the trick. To embrace Hynde in recent years, opt for the mocktail version.

| 2 ounces Patrón Añejo tequila or sparkling water | 2 ounces orange juice, freshly squeezed | Squeeze fresh lemon juice |
| | | Orange slice for garnishing |

Combine all ingredients except garnish in an ice-filled cocktail shaker. Strain into a tulip-shaped copita-style glass and garnish with the orange slice. Enjoy while sitting on the bed and looking at the sky while the clouds rearrange. "*Like the talk of the town.*"

1951

John Mellencamp's
BIG RED

SERVES 1

The Indiana-born singer, songwriter, and guitarist John Mellencamp is an icon in the heartland rock music scene. He formed his first band at age fourteen and would later move to New York City, where he was marketed as Johnny Cougar for a period by a manager before he became successful enough to require his true name be used. In the years to follow, the singer would become a champion of small communities and traditional American values, and release such rock staples as "Jack and Diane" (1982), "Hurts So Good" (1983), and "Pink Houses" (1983).

Today Mellencamp is a Rock and Roll Hall of Famer and a legend, but in his youth he was a heavy marijuana and alcohol user. In one interview he shared, "Oh, man! You think I have a temper now. You should have seen me when I was drunk. When I had a half pint of whiskey in me, I was a wild man. I was so obnoxious I couldn't stand myself. I was always getting beat up when I was drunk. I just had to quit."[125] So what has been fueling Mellencamp since he quit drinking in 1971? A backstage rider shows that a six-pack of IBC root beer and a six-pack of Coca-Cola were among his dressing room requirements, and one interviewer noted that his "hyperactivity is fueled by sodas and an endless supply of cigarettes"[126][127]—but what he really goes for is said to be Big Red soda. According to *Texas Monthly*, "Rock superstar John Cougar Mellencamp's only two vices are said to be cigarettes and Big Red," and the biography of Mellencamp written by Martin Torgoff notes that the drink, which he describes as "a fulsome soda with the sweet heavy taste of bubble gum that is only brewed in Texas," was a favorite of Mellencamp and his friends in their youth.[128] To channel the heartland singer, skip the hard stuff and enjoy his favorite bubble gum pop.

12-ounce can	Grilled cheese sandwich
Big Red soda	and french fries for pairing
	(optional)*

Drink the Big Red straight from the can or pour into a collins glass. Enjoy with grilled cheese and french fries while crooning songs that will became American staples.

*   According to Torgoff, Mellencamp and friends used to hang out at a local coffee shop where they could smoke cigarettes, drink Big Red, and eat grilled cheese sandwiches and fries.

1951

Sting's
FINE RED WINE

🍷 ⚡ SERVES 1

A singer, songwriter, bassist, and winner of seventeen Grammy Awards, Sting is an international rock icon whose sounds have seamlessly weaved together elements of new wave rock, punk, jazz, classical, reggae, and more. Sting was lead singer of the British rock band the Police from 1977 to 1984, and since then has enjoyed a successful solo career. Altogether Sting's music has sold more than 100 million albums, and he is responsible for such beloved songs as "Roxanne" (1978), "Message in a Bottle" (1979), and "Englishman in New York" (1988).

Like his music, Sting's taste in alcohol is highly refined. A backstage rider for one of his tours required "good quality red wine" and noted "cheap wines will not be accepted."[129] Today Sting even runs a Tuscan vineyard, Il Palagio, with his wife. The vineyard produces four red wines named after some of Sting's classic songs—because, according to Sting, "A wine is like a song—it has to tell a story."[130] And although Sting has spoken about having come from "a beer-drinking culture," today he prefers to drink only wine—either wine from Il Palagio or a Brunello di Montalcino Italian wine.[131]

To channel Sting, enjoy a high-quality red wine. For food pairings, note that Sting has revealed that "officially" his diet is very strict and healthy, but "unofficially: it's ice cream, chocolate, wine."[132]

5 ounces Il Palagio or Brunello di Montalcino wine

Dark chocolate or vanilla ice cream
for pairing (optional)

Pour wine into a red wine glass. Enjoy with a side of dark chocolate in the winter or vanilla ice cream in the summer, preferably accompanied by a Roxanne who wants to party all night.

Cyndi Lauper's
GIRLS JUST WANT TO HAVE ORGANIC WINE

SERVES 1

A Grammy, Tony, and Emmy Award–winning singer-songwriter, Cyndi Lauper has been performing for more than forty years and has sold more than fifty million albums. Among her hits are "Girls Just Want to Have Fun" (1983), "Time After Time" (1983), and "True Colors" (1986). Lauper is known for singing about strong, colorful women, and she's certainly one herself—known for her creative self-expression with a range of unusual hair colors, playful makeup, and jewelry, and for being an outspoken activist who has fought for LGBTQ rights, among other causes.

In Lauper's memoir she writes about dark times when she tried to soothe her pain with vodka, which she doesn't even have a taste for, but today the starlet is known for taking good care of herself and for being health conscious. In recent interviews she has shared how she rarely drinks anymore, and when she does, her preference is for organic or biodynamic wine. To channel her, then, take care to purchase wine from a trusted earth-friendly producer. And when you enjoy it, let loose. Sip, sing, and dance freely—and colorfully.

5 ounces organic or biodynamic wine

Pour the wine into a white or red wine glass. For best results enjoy while donning brightly colored locks and having fun. Repeat time after time.

1953

Pat Benatar's
STRAWBERRY ITALIAN SODA

SERVES 4

One of rock's leading ladies, Pat Benatar is a four-time Grammy Award winner who has sold more than thirty-five million albums worldwide. Her hits were on heavy rotation during the earliest days of MTV, when you would have been hard-pressed to watch an hour of the network and not see Benatar's videos for songs such as "Heartbreaker" (1979), "Hit Me With Your Best Shot" (1980), and "You Better Run" (1980), which was the second video ever played on MTV.

While many rock stars have lost their wits at times and been prone to overindulging, Benatar has always kept her cool. She shared in her memoir that drinking and drugs never appealed to her, writing: "I've always described myself as a very common person. I grew up without a lot of angst or internalized problems. I didn't sneak out after dark to raise hell and cause my parents any sleepless nights. No drinking. No drugging. You will never see my name in some scandal sheet. It's just not gonna happen." Where Benatar does indulge is with her cooking, and she's spoken frequently about her love for Italian food and cooking with produce she grows in her Maui garden, even once floating the idea of creating an Italian cookbook.

With the songstress's love for Italian cuisine and quality produce in mind, don't try to channel her with the same spirits other rockers require. Instead, go for an Italian cream soda. We think the sweet Benatar would be especially partial to this refreshing strawberry flavor.[133] If you, too, can use strawberries from your Maui garden, all the better.

1 cup diced
strawberries

½ cup
granulated sugar

1 tablespoon
lemon juice,
freshly squeezed

32 ounces
sparkling water

4 tablespoons
heavy cream

Whipped cream,
to taste

Strawberry slices
for garnishing

Combine the diced strawberries, sugar, lemon juice, and 1 cup still water in a saucepan and bring to a boil over high heat. Lower the heat to a simmer and cook for 10 minutes, then strain and cool to room temperature. Fill four tall soda glasses with ice and add a quarter of the sparkling water, strawberry mixture, and heavy cream to each. Stir to blend well, then top with whipped cream and the strawberry slices.

TIP: For extra Pat points, we suggest accompanying this with some soda bread muffins. Benatar and her husband posted a photo of their homemade ones on social media one fine St. Patrick's Day, and they looked absolutely delicious.

1954

David Lee Roth's
SCHLITZ MALT LIQUOR

SERVES 1

Van Halen, one of the preeminent hard rock groups of all time, was fronted by groundbreaking guitarist Eddie Van Halen and the outrageous, highly original singer David Lee Roth. The duo led the band's climb to the top of the charts with their song "Jump" (1984) and were also the masterminds of "Hot for Teacher" (1984) and "Unchained" (1981).

Onstage, Eddie's otherworldly guitar pyrotechnics and Roth's wild antics delighted fans—and behind the scenes the artists were equally over-the-top. In a wonky episode of Roth's YouTube series, *The Roth Show*, he gives an oral history of all the types of alcohol he's been stirred by over the years. Especially dear to his heart are Budweiser, which he notes is best enjoyed cold on a warm summer day with a side of roasted corn and barbecue, and Schlitz Malt Liquor, which he describes as "the drink of Van Halen, almost to our demise."[134]

The appreciation the band had for Schlitz Malt Liquor can be confirmed by one of their backstage riders, which called for four cases of it. Also noteworthy is the rider's call for M&M's, but (written in all caps and underlined), "ABSOLUTELY NO BROWN ONES."[135] News of this demand spread, with people interpreting the wording as a sign that the musicians had gone off the egomaniacal deep end. But the band's intent was to see if crews were paying close attention to the band's needs and expectations. In other words: if brown M&M's were in the bowl, how could the band be confident that the amplifiers were set up the way they needed them to be?

To invoke Van Halen, relax with your own ice-cold Schlitz Malt Liquor and pair its malty caramel notes with the band's approved candies.

| 16-ounce can | Red, orange, green, |
| Schlitz Malt Liquor | and yellow M&M's* for pairing |

Refrigerate beer until very cold, then pour into a stout glass. Serve with a side of colorful M&M's.

* Play it safe and also skip the blue, which hadn't been released at the time of the controversial rider request.

John Lydon's
RED STRIPE

SERVES 1

"I binge-drink, and I love it. I also love the hangover because
it reminds me not to do that again for a couple of months."
—John Lydon

J ohn Lydon, often known by his former stage name Johnny
Rotten, was a cofounder of the English punk rock band
the Sex Pistols and its lead singer, as well as the founder of
the band Public Image Ltd. Among his hits are the classic
Sex Pistols songs "Anarchy in the U.K." (1976), "God Save the
Queen" (1977), and "Pretty Vacant" (1977), and much to the
delight—or horror—of the public, the singer came to embody

a spirit of anarchy that would forever shape the rock music of the seventies. According to one colorful writer, Lydon "did not just espouse anarchy, he personified it, gyrating onstage like a broken marionette as he screeched against the pillars of polite society, while a hailstorm of spit rained in from the audience."[136]

What fueled the anarchist image we may never know, but we do know that Lydon is a beer drinker and has shared that his favorite brew is Red Stripe.[137] To channel him, enjoy a cold mug of the Jamaica-made ale.

──────────────────────────────

11.2-ounce bottle
Red Stripe, chilled

──────────────────────────────

Pour the Red Stripe into a tall beer mug or drink straight from the bottle. Rock hard.

Belinda Carlisle's
GREYHOUND

SERVES 1

The incredible singer-songwriter Belinda Carlisle established a name for herself as cofounder of the Go-Go's, the most successful all-girl band of the 1980s, before embarking on a solo career. With the Go-Go's she produced such high-energy hits as "Our Lips Are Sealed" (1981) and "We Got the Beat" (1981), and as a solo artist she gloriously sang such hits as "Heaven Is a Place on Earth" (1987), which would become her signature song, and "I Get Weak" (1987).

In Carlisle's beautifully penned memoir, she describes the behind-the-scenes partying she did as a rocker chick. Much of it was great fun, but it was also marked by cocaine and alcohol addictions, and today Carlisle doesn't drink. When she replaced her cocaine addiction with an alcohol addiction, she had a particular fondness for wine and in her book she shares how she would plan for days when she could drink heavily. One lighter section recounts how her time in the Go-Go's took her to Tokyo on multiple occasions, and there she would spend her days "drinking greyhounds and shopping in Harajuku."[138]

To channel the Carlisle from the height of the Go-Go's success, when she was living it up in Tokyo, enjoy a greyhound cocktail in its classic form. To channel Carlisle today, go for the mocktail version.

2 ounces vodka
or soda water

Lime wedge
for garnishing

4 ounces
grapefruit juice

Combine the vodka and grapefruit juice in a cocktail shaker, then pour into a collins glass filled with ice. Garnish with the lime wedge. If you were afraid before, don't be afraid anymore. If Heaven is a place on earth, this bright treat will light the way.

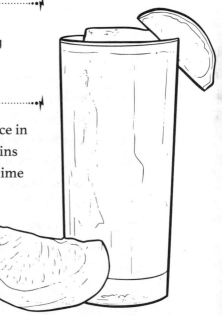

1958

Joan Jett's
CHERRY ALE

SERVES 1

A defining female force in rock and roll, a young Joan Jett was given a guitar as a Christmas gift from her parents and quickly connected with music. She took it for granted that those who told her that "girls don't play rock and roll" were out of their minds, and after her family's move to LA when she was a teenager, she became a founding member of the Runaways. But Jett would be entering a world where female musicians were expected to be sweet singer-songwriters and rock was thought to be a boys' game. As she noted in a documentary about her, she formed the Runaways with a belief that a girls' rock band would be "so cool and sexy because it's never been done" and that "everybody would love it." Unfortunately, "once they realized it was serious . . . the tables turned where it went from 'cute, sweet' to 'slut, whore.'"[139]

But for Jett, "Tell me I can't do something and you'll make sure I'm going to be doing it."[140] And she did. The Runaways would reach international acclaim. When disagreements and poor treatment led the band to break up, Jett embarked on a solo career and then founded Joan Jett and the Blackhearts. Today, she has paved the way for generations of girls to find a home in rock music. Her song repertoire includes such hits as "Cherry Bomb" (1976), the debut single she wrote for the Runaways that would reach the number six spot on the Billboard Hot 100 chart; "Bad Reputation" (1980); and "I Love Rock 'n Roll" (1981), her incredible cover of the song originally written for the UK band the Arrows.

In the period after the Runaways broke up, Jett had a rough time and she has shared how she drank and partied to help her cope. Today she takes good care of her health, is "close to vegan," and has shared, "I'll have an occasional drink, but I don't *drink*."[141] While Jett's drink of choice is uncertain, a wealth of photos from her younger years show her with a beer in hand. Given the success of "Cherry Bomb," we feel confident this cherry ale will do the trick in channeling the rock icon.

8 ounces
Belgian beer

4 sweet cherries,
pitted (reserve 1
for garnishing)

1 tablespoon
cherry juice

Squeeze fresh
lime juice

Thyme stem
for garnishing

Combine all ingredients except garnish with ice in a cocktail shaker. Strain into an ice-filled collins glass and garnish with the thyme stem and reserved cherry. Enjoy while professing your love for rock and roll and not giving a damn if you have a bad reputation.

Madonna's
DIRTY MARTINI

SERVES 1

Madonna, the queen of pop and rock whose spectacular, trailblazing career has spanned more than forty years, is a worldwide phenomenon. Among her dance-worthy hits are chart-topping classics including "Like a Virgin" (1984), "Material Girl" (1984), and "Like a Prayer" (1989). Together her sales of more than 300 million albums have earned her a Guinness World Record for best-selling female music artist of all time. She's also been named the greatest woman in music by VH1 and the greatest music video artist of all time by MTV and Billboard, as well as earned an artist achievement award from Billboard, twenty-eight Grammy nominations, and seven Grammy Awards.

With a background as a dancer, Madonna is known for being health conscious and eager to take good care of her body, but she's also shown that she indulges on occasion. A backstage rider of hers reveals that she sometimes travels with an acupuncturist, yoga instructor, and several personal chefs, and requires her meals to be vegan.[142] That said, she also once posted a photo of herself on Instagram that showed her in a gym surrounded by weights yet chugging Seventy One gin straight from the bottle. She captioned it: "Today's Workout."[143] When she's not drinking straight from the bottle, her favorite cocktail is thought to be a dirty martini, as she's shared photos of herself enjoying them on multiple occasions, including in one of her first posted photos and in the early months of the COVID pandemic when she captioned the photo "Quarantine Cocktail . . . 3 Olives—Extra Dry—Don't Bruise the Ice!"

2 ounces Seventy One gin	½ ounce dry vermouth	3 olives for garnishing
	¾ ounce olive brine	

Combine gin, vermouth, and olive brine in a cocktail shaker filled with ice. Do not, as Madonna instructs, bruise the ice (i.e. do not shake vigorously enough to create ice chips). Strain into a martini glass and garnish with the olives. Turn "Material Girl" to high and sip with grace like the music queen would.

1959

Morrissey's
PERONI NEGRONI

SERVES 1

The highly original, poetic singer-songwriter Morrissey first captured international acclaim as the lead singer for the Smiths and then embarked on a successful solo career. His interest in music led to roles in a number of small bands in the 1970s, and in 1978 he was introduced to then-fourteen-year-old Johnny Marr, who would reach out to him a few years later and sell him on the idea of starting a band together. That band would be the Smiths, and their unique indie- and punk-infused rock music would delight audiences throughout the 1980s, acquiring fans in their native UK and abroad. After the band split, Morrissey would focus on his own music and soon become a household name. Among his most well-known songs are "This Charming Man" (1983), "Suedehead" (1988), and "There Is a Light That Never Goes Out" (1992).

A free spirit, Morrissey has not been known to indulge in alcohol or drugs the way so many other rock icons do. Instead he is a self-described "tea-a-holic" who had a negative physical reaction the one day he tried to skip tea, and a passionate vegetarian who penned the Smiths' song "Meat Is Murder" (1985).[144] That said, he has been known to enjoy wine, vodka, and the vegan beer brand Peroni. To channel him, our recommendation is a Peroni cocktail—and given his poetic inclinations, we suggest a Peroni negroni.

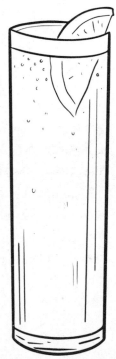

½ ounce gin

½ ounce Campari liqueur

½ ounce sweet vermouth

6 ounces Peroni Nastro Azzurro

Orange slice for garnishing

Combine gin, Campari, and sweet vermouth in an ice-filled collins glass, stir, and top with Peroni. Garnish with the orange slice. Sip while writing activist poetry you'll use as song lyrics.

1959

Susanna Hoffs's
COFFEE WITH CLOUDS

SERVES 1

S inger, songwriter, and guitarist Susanna Hoffs cofounded
the all-girl group the Bangles in 1981 with sisters Debbi and
Vicki Peterson. The Bangles would release several smash hits
and memorable videos, and Hoffs would later have a successful
solo career as well. Among her most memorable songs are
"Walk Like an Egyptian" (1986), "Manic Monday" (1986), and
"Eternal Flame" (1988).

Asked once what her secret to defying age is, Hoffs responded: "Listening to and playing music constantly. Mental stimulation. Exercise and moisturizer!"[145] A former dancer, Hoffs has also spoken often about the importance she places on exercise and healthy eating. She has said that she religiously takes daily outdoor walks and that she maintains a healthy diet. Hoffs gave up drinking alcohol in her fifties and is a vegetarian who sees importance in "eating whole foods whenever possible."[146] One vice Hoffs does partake in is regularly enjoying coffee, and she has often shared her love for the drink on social media—once on Twitter writing, "When in doubt, coffee."

Known for her keen choices of songs to cover, Hoffs sang Carly Simon's "You're So Vain" beautifully in 2009, including the line: "I had some dreams they were clouds in my coffee." Given her love for coffee and her awesome contributions to the music world, we think she deserves a coffee with clouds. Plus, this drink is your best aid in tackling a manic Monday.

8 ounces brewed coffee	½ teaspoon vanilla extract	2 large vegetarian marshmallows (avoid gelatin from animals)
Cream or milk of choice, to taste	Sugar, to taste	Cinnamon, to taste

Pour coffee into a large coffee mug, add cream, vanilla extract, and sugar, and stir. Drop in marshmallows and sprinkle with cinnamon.

Bono's
JACK ON THE ROCKS

SERVES 1

The epic front man for the band U2, singer-songwriter Bono has received twenty-two Grammy Awards and guided the band's rise to superstardom with his remarkable voice and range. He formed U2 in 1976 with the Edge, Adam Clayton, and Larry Mullen Jr., and the band's style has evolved throughout the years, incorporating elements of punk and pop into their sound. Today they've sold more than 170 million albums and their hits include such showstoppers as "I Still Haven't Found What I'm Looking For" (1987) from their epic *Joshua Tree* album, "One" (1992), and "Beautiful Day" (2000).

Bono has received a wealth of awards for his work and service as a musician and philanthropist—but he's known to be able to kick back, and thankfully didn't suffer from the addictions that plagued Clayton. A look at a U2 backstage rider reveals the band required multiple different kinds of beer and wine, as well as champagne, port or sherry, tequila, vodka, and "Jack Daniel's Black"—a reference to JD's classic No. 7 whiskey.[147] We can assume that the whiskey was for Bono, as it's believed to be his drink of choice. In one interview, when asked if he likes being intoxicated, the Christian artist raised a finger and responded: "'Tis better to be drunk on the spirit; however, a bottle of Jack Daniel's is sometimes handier."[148] To channel Bono, if you're bold enough to do so, go with a simple Jack on the rocks.

1 ½ ounces Jack Daniel's Old No. 7 whiskey

Pour the whiskey into an ice-filled highball glass. Turn up the U2 and let Bono's warm, hypnotic voice envelop and inspire you. See if this helps you find what you're looking for.

The Beach Boys'
FROZEN BAHAMA MAMA

SERVES 1

Hailing from suburban California, the Beach Boys—originally composed of Wilson brothers Brian, Carl, and Dennis, their cousin Mike Love, and high school friend Al Jardine—were expert vocal harmonists who produced countless hits including "Surfin' U.S.A." (1963), "California Girls" (1966), "Good Vibrations" (1966), and "Wouldn't It Be Nice" (1966). Today Love is the only original band member who continues to tour under the band's name. In his eighties, Love has said: "If you're healthy and if people want to hear you perform, there is no reason to retire."[149] A practitioner of transcendental meditation, which he learned from the Maharishi Mahesh Yogi while in India with the Beatles, Love is a rock and roller known for his juice cleanses and reportedly once went on an apple juice fast, carrying a two-gallon jug of apple juice everywhere he went. His fellow Beach Boys bandmates, however, partook in the great liquid enabler.

Let yourself be inspired by "Kokomo" (1988) and relax with a frozen bahama mama. Enjoy as a juice, as Love would have taken it, or harder like the other boys would have preferred.

½ ounce rum or pineapple juice

½ ounce grenadine

½ ounce coconut rum or coconut juice

Pineapple wedge for garnishing

1 ounce orange juice, freshly squeezed

Cherry for garnishing

Combine all ingredients except garnishes with 1 cup ice in a blender and blend until the drink reaches the consistency of a slushy. Pour into a poco grande glass and add garnishes, plus a paper umbrella to really get into that tropical mood and emit good vibrations.

1961

Kim Deal's
GIN FIZZ

SERVES 1

Indie rock star Kim Deal and her twin sister, Kelley, started playing music as kids and formed a folk band in their teenage years. In 1986 Deal answered an ad to join the newly forming band the Pixies and began playing bass and singing for them. She would soon become the band's front woman and help secure a cult fanbase. In 2013 Deal officially parted ways with the Pixies to focus on her other band, the Breeders, which she had created in 1989 and which she had focused on during Pixies breakups over the years. Kelley would join the band, and today they are a punk rock sister duo to be reckoned with. Among Deal's most well-known songs are "Gigantic" (1988), "Silver" (1989), and "Cannonball" (1993).

Both Deal sisters are sober today, but were known to indulge in their younger years. Although Deal's drink of choice when she partook isn't known, she has shared that when she and Kelley were backup singers, men would buy them gin fizzes.[150] We can't get behind a gin fizz in this context, but we can certainly get behind making one for yourself to channel Deal in her youth, or enjoying one sans gin to channel Deal today.

3 ounces club soda
(reserve 1 ounce
for topping)

2 ounces
gin (optional;
or 2 additional
ounces club soda)

1 ounce lemon
juice, freshly
squeezed

½ ounce
simple syrup

Lemon slice
for garnishing

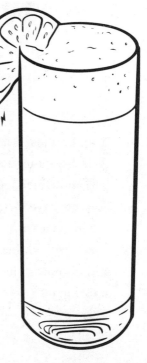

Combine all ingredients except garnish with ice in a cocktail shaker and shake until cold. Strain into an ice-filled collins glass, top with remaining club soda, and garnish with the lemon slice. Enjoy between indie rock songs.

1962

Jon Bon Jovi's
HAMPTON WATER ROSÉ

SERVES 1

Jon Bon Jovi is a singer, songwriter, heartthrob, and front man of the eponymous rock band Bon Jovi, which he formed in 1983 and which today has sold more than 100 million albums. Top hits have included such iconic songs as "Runaway" (1984), "Livin' on a Prayer" (1986), and "You Give Love a Bad Name" (1986), and while Bon Jovi's star status has risen over the years and his hair styles have changed, he's always remained a steady, stable icon.

When it comes to drinking, Bon Jovi's a reliable wine drinker and skips the harder stuff. In one interview he shared, "I don't drink hard alcohol. Red, whites, and rosé are all I ever drink" and joked that while he doesn't drink before performing, afterward he'll be "standing next to the bottle."[151] This appreciation for wine is further documented by a Bon Jovi backstage rider, which has no hard liquor listed, only wine. Bon Jovi and his son have even started their own wine company.[152] The wine is a French rosé and Bon Jovi has shared that he would have called it "Pink Juice," but his son's suggested name for the wine, Hampton Water, won out.

To channel the legend, get your hands on a bottle of his rosé. Keep things easy while drinking and avoid drunk dialing any exes or starting fights with loved ones. You wouldn't want to give love a bad name.

5 ounces Hampton Water rosé or other high-quality rosé, chilled

Pour the chilled wine into a white wine glass. Enjoy while letting your long locks flow, singing your heart out, and smiling a one-hundred-watt smile.

Courtney Love's
PÉTRUS

SERVES 1

The lead singer of the rock band Hole, Courtney Love is known for her superb vocals, her wild character and antics, and her marriage to Kurt Cobain. Love's musical career began in the late 1980s, after she taught herself to play guitar and then started the band Hole. Hole would quickly gain a reputation for vibrant performances and intense music, and Love would produce such hits as "Celebrity Skin" (1998), "Awful" (1999), and "Nobody's Daughter" (2010).

Love and Cobain would marry in 1992, but Cobain would take his own life just two years later. The Nirvana front man was known to have a heroin addiction and Love would become known as a drug abuser as well, with drugs affecting her behavior and causing wild and very public outbursts. Today Love says she is sober, and while we can't recommend a drug binge to channel the eccentric star, we can recommend a single glass of the high-end wine she enjoys, if you can afford it. The singer has shared that she was never much of a drinker, but that Bono once gave her a bottle of Pétrus in France and the wine, according to Love, "gets you so stoned in a really opiated way, like you'd just taken a Vicodin."[153] She thought the wine was the cure to getting drug addicts off drugs until a month later when she "found out it cost $12K!"[154] If your paycheck allows you to go for the drink the singer enjoyed, by all means do so—and let us know what it's like. Otherwise, try our suggested substitution.

5 ounces Pétrus or other
high-quality
French red from Bordeaux

Pour the wine into a red wine glass and drink while releasing inhibitions, singing loudly, letting your hair down, dancing freely, and interrupting others' interviews.

TIP: If you prefer to follow Love's sober path today, swap the wine for lemon water, which she drinks regularly and has called "the key to life."

1964

Eddie Vedder's
PINOT NOIR

SERVES 1

L ead vocalist and guitarist for Pearl Jam Eddie Vedder was
recruited to join the band on its formation in 1990 and
would shape the sound of the band's alternative rock, eventually leading to their sales of more than eighty-five million
albums, an induction into the Rock and Roll Hall of Fame, and,
later, Vedder's success as a solo artist as well. Among his top
hits are "Black" (1991), "Alive" (1991), and "Jeremy" (1992).

Onstage, Vedder provides exhilarating performances and
often has a bottle with him that he drinks out of—and for years
its contents have been the subject of speculation. The answer
to what he is drinking was finally revealed to *Rolling Stone*, with

Vedder sharing that it's red wine, and research by *Wine Spectator* magazine uncovered that the wine is Siduri Van der Kamp Vineyard's pinot noir, which the winery sends to Vedder in bottles without labels.[155] To channel Vedder, we recommend going for the good stuff, but a label-free bottle of another high-quality pinot should do the job too.

ᴴ•••ᴴ

5 ounces Siduri Van der Kamp Vineyard Pinot Noir or other high-quality pinot noir

ᴴ•••ᴴ

Remove the label from the wine bottle and drink straight from the bottle while dressed in jeans and flannel and rocking hard as you delight audiences worldwide, or leave the label and enjoy from a red wine glass while Pearl Jam classics set the mood.

Lenny Kravitz's
DOM PÉRIGNON

SERVES 1

When Lenny Kravitz began playing music professionally in the mid-1980s, the biracial artist faced pressure from record labels to make his music for either a black or white audience, but Kravitz wanted to play what felt authentic and fresh and not be boxed in. The result was a collection of hits that fused rock, funk, R & B, blues, soul, and other elements, and a loyal audience of fans worldwide. Today Kravitz's hits include "It Ain't Over 'Til It's Over" (1991), which reached the number two spot on the Billboard Hot 100 list, "Are You Gonna Go My Way" (1993), and "Fly Away" (1998).

As a child Kravitz moved from New York City to LA, and today he splits his time between a Paris mansion, where he lives in luxury, and an organic farm in the Bahamas, where he lives with very few items. In addition to being a rock star, he is also a fashion icon and an activist. As additional evidence that he can live between multiple worlds, Kravitz has described himself as a champagne hippie.[156] He embraces values associated with hippie culture, but has always appreciated a glass of champagne and today is even a creative director for the iconic French champagne house Dom Pérignon. In one interview, when asked his fondest memory of drinking champagne, he shared: "I still remember one evening drinking 1964 Dom Pérignon at Château Dom Pérignon. I spent that evening in front of the fireplace with a friend. It was extravagant. I've always been a champagne lover." As to how he drinks it, he responded: "I like to go high and low, that's the beauty of it. Before this interview I was sat here, sipping champagne and eating my vegan pizza—it was perfect. You don't need to do anything too extravagant."[157] For us, channeling a music legend through champagne and vegan pizza truly does sound perfect.

4 ounces
Dom Pérignon, chilled

1 slice vegan pizza
for pairing (optional)

Pour Dom Pérignon into a champagne flute. Enjoy with a side of vegan pizza while remembering that it's always okay to be more than one thing and you're not alone if you've ever had a dream that someday you would fly away.

1965

Björk's
ALL IS FULL
OF LOVE SPRITZ

SERVES 1

The avant-garde Icelandic singer-songwriter Björk's fusion of electronic, rock, pop, and other styles with her enchanting, breathy vocals has captivated audiences worldwide. The artist's music career began at eleven and she would later become the lead singer for the Sugarcubes, performing with them until 1992, when she embarked on a solo career. Among her beloved hits are "Hyperballad" (1995), "Army of Me" (1995), and "All Is Full of Love" (1999). She is also a film icon, having starred in *Dancer in the Dark*, which earned her a Best Actress Golden Globe, and a style icon known for such iconic statements as her swan dress at the Academy Awards.

When it comes to liquid fuel, Björk is known to enjoy in moderation. A backstage rider for one tour required a half-bottle of Rémy Martin VSOP cognac, a bottle of red wine, and a bottle of chilled champagne, and she's been vocal about her appreciation for vodka. Reportedly, she once shared: "I come from a country where, from the age of fifteen, you drink a liter of vodka every Friday, straight from the bottle. I watch my granddad and my grandmother, and it's my pattern. It's a release that's been going on in my family for a thousand years. Purely from alcohol is how people lose themselves and put their little policeman off shift and run riot. I actually need it in my life."[158] To channel Björk (and her family), enjoy this sweet spritz inspired by a recipe from the Icelandic vodka company Reyka.

2 ounces Reyka vodka
3 ounces raspberry and rhubarb tonic water
Strawberry for garnishing

Stir the vodka and tonic water together in a large white wine glass filled with ice. Garnish with the strawberry. Allow yourself to become filled with love and dance freely in the dark.

1966

Janet Jackson's
GRAPEFRUIT COSMO

SERVES 1

The remarkable singer-songwriter and dance icon Janet Jackson was the tenth and youngest child of the musical family the Jacksons, making her the little sister of the boys, including Michael, in the Jackson 5. At age seven Janet would begin performing too, and at age sixteen she would release her first album and begin to make a name for herself as a solo artist. Today Jackson is a global superstar who has sold more than 100 million albums and is responsible for such hits as "Nasty" (1986), "Black Cat" (1990), and "That's the Way Love Goes" (1993).

On Jackson's rise to the top, she battled racism and sexism and dealt with personal struggles, but she doesn't believe in abusing alcohol or drugs to avoid one's problems. She has shared how she has never tried drugs and is a light drinker, in one interview revealing: "As far as drinking, I've had a brandy Alexander . . . . They're so incredible, but they don't affect you until you stand up. I was out once and had wine and I got sick to my stomach, and I vowed I would never drink again. . . . [In the house] we have wine and champagne when we have dinners, or when guests come over."[159] But while Jackson doesn't drink much, she has been known to enjoy the occasional cocktail; an article in *People* magazine, for example, shares a time when she was spotted enjoying grapefruit cosmos with her girlfriends at an LA restaurant.[160]

We can certainly get behind letting a grapefruit cosmo be the drink of choice when one occasionally indulges. To channel Jackson, try this sweet version.

1 ounce vodka

½ ounce triple sec

½ cup ruby red grapefruit juice

1 teaspoon lime juice, freshly squeezed

Grapefruit slice for garnishing

Fill a cocktail shaker with ice and mix all ingredients except garnish together in it. Strain into a martini glass and garnish with the grapefruit slice. Best enjoyed while dressed to kill and knowing you've got what it takes to rise to the top.

1967

Chicago's
SATURDAY CABERNET

SERVES 1

Chicago first formed in 1967 and today the band is one of the longest-performing and best-selling bands in the United States, with thirty-seven albums and sales of over forty million copies to their name. Original members Robert Lamm, Lee Loughnane, and James Pankow continue to perform with the band, respectively playing the keyboard, trumpet, and trombone that have defined the band's unique "rock and roll with horns" sound. Among Chicago's classic songs are "25 or 6 to 4" (1970), which embraced the rare talent of guitarist Terry Kath, "Saturday in the Park" (1972), and "Hard to Say I'm Sorry" (1982).

In a documentary about the band, members and associates revealed their taste for partying, drinking, and drugs in their youth. Loughnane recalled, "I was drinking all the time . . . . Dumb kids thinking we're indestructible, you know, live forever." Pankow noted, "Because you could get away with so much, you did get away with so much." And Lamm spoke about the drugs the band members used at a ranch retreat, sharing: "I think that when you put young guys with too much money together in an isolated venue . . . it's a recipe for disaster, and it was." On one tour, the band had a faux phone booth installed on their set and they would pop into it to do quick lines of cocaine without audiences realizing. They dubbed it their "Snortatorium."[161]

But while the band members have spoken prolifically about their drug use and partying, when it comes to drinking they've shown their tastes tend to be pretty vanilla, with preferences being given toward beer or a good wine. In one interview, Pankow shared: "Generally, I lean toward lush cab-centric reds."[162] And given that it's been said that the members of Chicago, like fine wine, get better with age, we think this is appropriate. Perfection would have to be the "Saturday in the Park" sung about by Lamm with a bottle of aged cabernet on your picnic blanket.

5 ounces Château Lafite
Rothschild Cabernet Sauvignon blend*

Pour the wine into a red wine glass. Turn on "Saturday in the Park" and dance, laugh, and enjoy, preferably in the company of longtime friends who would also dig changing the world.

* This wine is what Pankow calls the "premier grand cru."[163] If a bottle of it, which can go for up to fifteen hundred dollars, is out of your price range, go for something more affordable and turn the music up an extra notch.

1967

Three Dog Night's
MIGHTY FINE WINE
AND CHEESE

SERVES 1

Three Dog Night was formed in 1967 by singers Danny Hutton, Cory Wells, and Chuck Negron, and would go on to become a classic rock sensation. The band would have dozens of hits, among them the ultra-catchy "Joy to the World" (1970), which was originally written by Hoyt Axton, and which Hutton and Wells thought too childish to record until pushed to do so by Negron, as well as "Mama Told Me (Not to Come)" (1970) and "An Old Fashioned Love Song" (1971).

Today Hutton is the only founding member of the band still performing in it, as Negron left the band following a serious heroin addiction, which he has since recovered from, and Wells left following a serious illness, which would take his life. But during the band's peak creative years, Hutton and Negron were known for their wild partying and eagerness to indulge in drinking, drugs, and love making. Wells, a family man, was reportedly more disciplined.

With age, however, it seems that Hutton no longer partakes as he once did; his indulgences today are wine, beer, and brie cheese according to one interview.[164] To channel Three Dog Night, enjoy a serving of the "very fine wine" the band made waves helping their friend Jeremiah the bullfrog enjoy, and pay homage to Hutton's refined taste with a classy side of brie.

5 ounces Chardonnay, chilled
Brie for pairing

Pour the Chardonnay into a white wine glass and let its bright acidity excite your taste buds in between bites of brie. Make sure to be kind to any bullfrogs that pass by as you sing joy to the world without reservation.

EPIC ROCK CLUBS TO DRINK, DANCE, AND PERFORM IN: CBGB, WHISKY A GO GO, AND THE 100 CLUB

Music history has been defined by the performances of the up-and-coming and established stars who've graced the stages of dark, loud, smoky, beer-soaked venues from New York to LA, London, and beyond—throwing back drinks and then riveting fans.

In New York City's East Village, CBGB opened in 1973, and while its letters announced it as a home for country, bluegrass, and blues from day one, it would soon welcome punk, new wave, experimental, and all shades of rock as well. Memorable nights would include performances from the Ramones, Blondie, the Patti Smith Group, Joan Jett, Guns N' Roses, and more, until its closing in 2006. In West Hollywood, Whisky a Go Go opened on the Sunset Strip in 1964. The club popularized go-go dancing, was a launching pad for a wealth of bands, and would become a music landmark inducted into the Rock and Roll Hall of Fame. Among its featured performers have been Led Zeppelin, Fleetwood Mac, Alice Cooper, AC/DC, Kiss, Chicago, No Doubt, and the Doors. In London, Oxford Street's 100 Club opened with the name Macks in 1942 and was renamed in 1964. Its acts have included the Who, the Sex Pistols, and the Rolling Stones. Honorable mentions should also be given to New York's Cafe Wha?, West Hollywood's Troubadour, and Manchester's Haçienda. As anyone who has been to a live show knows well, there is something intoxicating, almost otherworldly, about being surrounded by music. Streamed tunes or physical albums can delight, but there is nothing quite like a live show.

1969

Dave Grohl's
DEER AND BEER

SERVES 1

Dave Grohl has been an integral part of two of rock's most influential bands. In the early nineties, he was the drummer for Nirvana. After Kurt Cobain's death, Grohl started the Foo Fighters, writing all the songs and playing all the instruments on the band's debut album in 1995 and then bringing in more members. Today the Foo Fighters have won twelve Grammy Awards and sold an estimated twenty million albums. Their songs include "Everlong" (1997), "Aurora" (1999), and "Times Like These" (2002).

Grohl remains a top rocker, but the demands of his personal life, including parenting, sometimes have him drinking up to four pots of coffee a day. (A *Washington Post* reporter once called him "a back-aching, coffee-guzzling, minivan-driving classic rocker."[165]) To get pumped for shows and turn on the version of himself who enchants fans every time, the musician has long relied on an hours-long drinking ritual before every show. The ritual begins with taking three Advil ninety minutes before a performance, drinking a Coors Light sixty minutes before, having a Jägermeister shot fifty minutes before, and then moving on to more Coors Lights and more shots.[166]

We're not sure the human body is designed for what Grohl imbibes, so instead we recommend channeling him through Jägermeister's deer and beer cocktail.[167] Use Grohl's beloved Coors Light for the best effect, and save the Advil for the morning after.

| 1 ½ ounces Jägermeister, ice cold | 12-ounce bottle Coors Light, cold |

Pour the Jägermeister into a chilled beer mug, fill with the Coors Light, and stir to combine. Enjoy while sipping slowly and pensively, as it's times like these you learn to live again.

Gwen Stefani's
HUGO

SERVES 1

Singer-songwriter and three-time Grammy Award-winning modern-day pop rock icon Gwen Stefani was the cofounder of No Doubt and its lead singer and songwriter before embarking on a successful solo career. With No Doubt, Stefani was responsible for such hits as "Just a Girl" (1995), "Spiderwebs" (1995), and "Don't Speak" (1996), and her solo career has produced "Hollaback Girl" (2004), "Cool" (2004), and "What You Waiting For?" (2004).

According to Stefani, her parents were very strict and conservative and didn't drink, but today she and husband Blake Shelton enjoy occasionally indulging. In one interview about their Christmas rituals, she shared: "We all drink wine mainly, but we also do this one drink, I don't know what they're called, but my friend that's English turned me on to them. It has mint and prosecco and this liquor that goes in it."[168] The journalist followed Stefani's quote with a note that "Intense Googling could not uncover what the hell Gwen was talking about, but we think it's a hugo"—and we agree! Thus to invoke the singer, set your table with a delicious hugo cocktail and enjoy the sweet taste of elderflower mixing with mint and prosecco.

1 mint sprig and 3 mint leaves for garnishing

¼ ounce St~Germain elderflower liqueur

8 ounces prosecco, chilled

Soda water for topping

Lime wedge for garnishing

Bruise the mint sprig and place it in an ice-filled white wine glass. Add the elderflower liqueur and prosecco and stir gently. Top with soda water and garnish with the lime wedge and mint leaves. No doubt this is what you were waiting for. Enjoy while walking into a spiderweb. If there are any phone calls let them leave a message and you'll call them back.

AC/DC's
CHOCOLATE MILK MARTINI

SERVES 1

The Australian headbanging band AC/DC was formed in 1973 by Scottish guitar-playing brothers Angus and Malcolm Young. Known for their hard riffs and catchy lyrics, the band is responsible for such hits as "Highway to Hell" (1979), "You Shook Me All Night Long" (1980), and "Thunderstruck" (1990), and has sold more than 200 million albums worldwide.

As the band's lineup changed over the years, Angus Young remained the only constant, and adoring fans delighted over his schoolboy stage outfits, duckwalk, and compelling presence. But while Young has sung about drinking, most memorably with "Have a Drink On Me" (1980)—and the band has even licensed its name to a collection of tequilas and premium lagers under the label Thunderstruck—Young himself is unlikely to partake. Instead, he favors chocolate milk. A peek at one of the band's riders reveals that band bus 1 required whole milk, band bus 2 required skim milk, and the band's common area required milk as well. We know Young's true preference was chocolate milk, though, as both he and former band members have spoken about this.

To channel AC/DC, enjoy this chocolate milk martini. Have it virgin as Angus Young would, or go with the version that the rest of the band's current and former members would likely be more drawn to.

2 ounces chocolate milk	3 ounces vanilla vodka (optional)	Cocoa powder for garnishing
	1 ½ ounces crème de cacao	

Stir all ingredients except cocoa powder together in a chilled martini glass. Garnish with a sprinkle of cocoa powder. Make noise, roll around, hit the ground, take another swig, and have another drink.

TIP: For bonus points, enjoy with Young's favorite sandwich: a chip butty sandwich composed of french fries and a burger. About this sandwich, he once noted in a Reddit "Ask Me Anything" forum: "It's got rock and roll written all over it. If you said to me, 'Would you rather have a chip butty or dine with the president,' I'd say the chip butty and he'd probably follow suit."[169]

1973

Journey's
ORANGE CREAMSICLE

🥤⚡ SERVES 1

Journey's years with singer-songwriter Steve Perry as their lead singer—1977 to 1987 and 1995 to 1998—were their most successful and produced such iconic hits as "Don't Stop Believin'" (1981), which became the band's signature song, a top ten hit worldwide, and the most-paid-for digitally downloaded song of the twentieth century, as well as "Faithfully" (1983) and "When You Love a Woman" (1996).

Conflict with band members and Perry's personal issues would lead him to take a break from Journey and eventually leave the band, but he found vodka a friend to lean on during difficult times. In one interview he noted, "I wouldn't drink onstage, but I'd get offstage, and when I got in the bus, there'd be a chilled bottle of whatever vodka I was drinking, and I'd start plowin' into it. And I'd sleep, and I'd wake up, go do the gig, and the same thing would happen all over again."[170]

We're glad Perry has overcome his alcohol addiction, and separately delighted in seeing a backstage rider of the band's from 1991, a period when Perry wasn't with them. The rider required Stewart's Orange 'n Cream soda as one of their very specific needs for the band bus and lounge room.[171] If your mouth also waters at the thought of Perry and the band back together, you too may enjoy this mix from both worlds. We know this cocktail and that dream are both a little out there, but hey, don't stop believin'.

1 ounce whipped cream vodka, chilled

1 ounce half-and-half

1 ounce Stewart's Orange 'n Cream soda, chilled

Splash orange juice, freshly squeezed

Orange slice for garnishing

Mix chilled vodka and soda in a cocktail shaker and stir in half-and-half and orange juice. Pour into a collins glass filled with ice and garnish with the orange slice.

1974

Squeeze's
BRANDY SOUR

SERVES 1

English rock band Squeeze rose to fame in the seventies and eighties when singer and guitarist Glenn Tilbrook and singer Chris Difford were dubbed "the new Lennon and McCartney." The band has taken breaks over the years, but continues to perform today. A huge success in the UK, the new wave rock band acquired a devoted following in the States as well, with fans hungrily purchasing albums featuring such hits as "Pulling Mussels (from the Shell)" (1980), "Tempted" (1981), and "Black Coffee in Bed" (1982).

While a black coffee in bed might do the trick to channel the British legends, Tilbrook and Difford were known for indulging in the hard stuff during their peak creative years. In fact, Difford once shared how his daughters were going through his touring archives and discovered a backstage rider that required two bottles of brandy on Mondays, two bottles of vodka on Tuesdays, and other liquors to fill the week. We can't speak to what the band members' drink of choice was, but in the memoir of Alex James, bass player for the band Blur, he recalls a very drunk and happy Tilbrook frolicking with Blur musician Graham Coxon. The two were "drinking a bottle of brandy, doing handstands, and knocking everything over."[172]

With this enjoyment of brandy in mind, we recommend channeling the band members through this brandy sour. Do keep in mind, though, that they once titled a song "I Won't Ever Go Drinking Again" (1985). If you intend to drink again, probably best to keep to just one, or at least plan for black coffee in bed the next morning.

2 ounces brandy

1 ounce lemon juice, freshly squeezed

4 drops bitters

½ ounce simple syrup

Splash soda water

Lime wedge for garnishing

Combine brandy and lemon juice in a cocktail shaker, then pour into a highball glass filled with ice. Stir in bitters and simple syrup, top with a splash of soda water, and garnish with the lime wedge.

1975

Fergie's
FERGATINI

SERVES 1

Fergie began her career as a child doing acting and voiceover work, rose to fame after joining the Black Eyed Peas, and later embarked on a solo career. Her superb dance-friendly music fuses elements of hip hop, rock, and pop, and she has received eight Grammy Awards and nine Billboard Music Awards. Among her hit songs are "My Humps" (2005), "Fergalicious" (2006), and "Big Girls Don't Cry" (2007). In addition to music, she is known for continuing to act and for her work as a fashion designer.

Often seen with a cocktail in hand at a gala, Fergie is a partial owner of Voli Vodka, which is marketed as a "low-calorie vodka." She was introduced to the company by the rapper Pitbull, another partial owner. Since joining the company, she has shared drink recipes using Voli on multiple platforms and even hosted a charity cocktail party where the drinks embraced the vodka. One of the drinks at the party, the Fergatini, was made from Voli Light, lime juice, and cranberry juice—and, according to Fergie, the drink is only eighty-two calories.[173] To channel Fergie, enjoy a Fergatini yourself. If it proves a good way to stick to a low-calorie diet that supports a physique capable of killer dance moves, you'll find us at the bar.

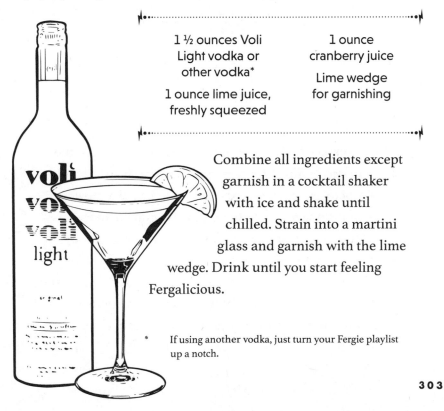

1 ½ ounces Voli Light vodka or other vodka*

1 ounce lime juice, freshly squeezed

1 ounce cranberry juice

Lime wedge for garnishing

Combine all ingredients except garnish in a cocktail shaker with ice and shake until chilled. Strain into a martini glass and garnish with the lime wedge. Drink until you start feeling Fergalicious.

* If using another vodka, just turn your Fergie playlist up a notch.

1977

Shakira's
GREEN BERRY SMOOTHIE

SERVES 1

The Colombian singer-songwriter Shakira is one of the most successful Latin American recording artists and is widely beloved on an international stage. With a powerful voice, extraordinary vocal range, and killer dance moves, Shakira began performing professionally as a young teenager, recording her debut album with Sony at just thirteen. She would break through first in the Latin market and then across the globe, releasing songs in both Spanish and English. Today she has won three Grammy Awards, twelve Latin Grammy

Awards, and multiple Billboard Music Awards and Guinness World Records, and has sold more than eighty million albums. Among her hit songs are "Whenever, Wherever" (2001), "Hips Don't Lie" (2005), and "She Wolf" (2009).

Shakira has spoken about her love for food in moderation, but is not known to indulge in alcohol or even caffeine. Reportedly her abstention from alcohol is tied to the death of her brother when she was a young child as the result of a drunk driver. To channel her, skip the booze and go for the berry smoothie that her trainer has shared is part of Shakira's breakfast on a typical day. The drink was described as a "smoothie with berries, plant protein, greens, or a green powder" and we think this green berry smoothie perfectly fits the bill.[174]

1 ¼ cups almond milk

½ cup raspberries

½ cup blueberries

1 banana

1 cup spinach

1 scoop vanilla plant protein powder

Combine all ingredients with ice in a blender and blend until smooth. Pour into a large drinking glass and add a reusable straw. Enjoy whenever, wherever.

1978

Karen O's
PATRÓN AND TONIC

SERVES 1

Singer, songwriter, and eccentric front woman for the Yeah
Yeah Yeahs Karen O has been said to exuberantly represent
and entertain fans through her "weirdo outsider artist's
multi-channel multicultural creative identity well ahead of
descendants like Lady Gaga, M.I.A., and Grimes."[175] She was
born in South Korea, but grew up in New Jersey and moved to
NYC for school, which is where she would cofound the powerful indie rock band the Yeah Yeah Yeahs in 2000. In the years
to follow, the band would release such hits as "Maps" (2003),
"Zero" (2009), and "Heads Will Roll" (2009).

With the band's rise, Karen O would come to embody a
certain kind of wild and free rock icon. At shows she would

become known for downing one beer and pouring two others all over herself and her mic stand—much to the delight of a roaring crowd. Joe Levy called it "unhinged, deeply hilarious, completely spontaneous behavior."[176]

In addition to beer, Karen O has shared that she likes to indulge in tequila when she's letting loose, and champagne when she's looking to tone things down a notch. We say if you're looking to channel the singer, go all out, but perhaps enjoy a mixed drink instead of the tequila straight up— unless it's one of those nights and you, too, want to end up covered in beer.

2 ounces Patrón Silver tequila
3 ounces tonic water
Lime wedge for garnishing

Stir Patrón and tonic water together in an ice-filled highball glass and garnish with the lime wedge. Best enjoyed while sporting a miniskirt, smeared lipstick, and glittery eyeshadow, and dancing like a wild woman.

1979

Pink's
JAMESON McCREE

SERVES 1

The edgy icon Pink is a consistent, steady force in today's music scene. She began performing as a teenager and got her professional start as an R & B artist before transitioning to the pop rock that defines her music today. Now nearly twenty years into her career, Pink has sold more than 135 million albums and won three Grammy Awards, was awarded a Billboard Woman of the Year Award, and is responsible for such songs as "So What" (2008), "Try" (2012), and "Just Give Me a Reason" (2013). Her acrobatic aerial dancing and unique, raspy voice have become her trademarks, and while her lyrics express a distinct furor, she is known for having it together.

We can certainly get behind Pink's ability to enjoy alcohol without succumbing to the addictions of so many other music legends. And she is known to have a strong palate and to enjoy a variety of different types of libations. For example, she owns a small Santa Barbara vineyard that produces Two Wolves wine and has shared that she has a passion for wine growing. She also has a passion for a Western Pomeranian amaro and once gave the Zinzow distillery a major boost in sales by posting her (unsolicited) love for the product on social media. And then there's the fact that she named her son Jameson, in part due to the love that she and her husband have for the whiskey brand.[177]

To channel Pink, by all means go for the Western Pomeranian spirit or her wine if you can get your hands on a bottle—otherwise, go for a drink embracing the easy-to-find Jameson. Though Pink has been seen drinking it on the rocks, we recommend a Jameson McCree as the cocktail is her rosy hue.

1 ½ ounces Jameson whiskey	½ ounce raspberry liqueur	½ ounce simple syrup
1 ounce cranberry juice	½ ounce lemon juice, freshly squeezed	¼ cup raspberries (reserve a few for garnishing)

Combine all ingredients in a blender until smooth, then pour into an ice-filled highball glass and garnish with the reserved raspberries. Enjoy while alerting everyone that you're a rock star with rock moves. *Na-na-na-na, na-na, na . . . .*

1981

Beyoncé's
ARMAND DE BRIGNAC

SERVES 1

Modern-day music royalty Beyoncé was born in Houston and began performing as a child. In 1997 her band would change their name to Destiny's Child and the R & B group would rise to fame, with Beyoncé a star member until 2002, when she embarked on a solo career. Today the starlet is one of the most popular recording artists of our time, a multi-platinum, record-breaking artist with a remarkable seventy-nine Grammy nominations and twenty-eight wins. Among her hits are "Crazy in Love" (2003), which features her husband, Jay-Z, "Single Ladies (Put a Ring on It)" (2008), which won three Grammys, and "Halo" (2009).

To channel the singer, pop open a bottle of bubbly and sing to release your inner Queen Bee. It's known that Beyoncé and Jay-Z are especially partial to Armand de Brignac champagne—Jay-Z is an investor in the brand, and the couple took bottles of it with them when they attended the 2020 Golden Globes. Note, however, that a bottle of the French champagne can cost around three hundred dollars. So if you're able to splurge, by all means go ahead, otherwise go with a more affordably priced bottle of bubbly and just kick the music up a notch.

6 ounces Armand de Brignac
or other champagne, chilled

Pour the champagne into a champagne flute. Sip while walking into a room like you own the place and we're sure you'll have us at hello. *"Hello, hello. 'Cause you had me at hello."*

Metallica's
CROWN ROYAL
AND GINGER

SERVES 1

"The first second we were together, they raided everything there was out of the liquor cabinet in my house. They drank all the bottles down without even using glasses." —Megaforce Records owner Jon Zazula speaking about Metallica

Formed in 1981 by singer and guitarist James Hetfield and drummer Lars Ulrich, Metallica grew to become a hard rock and heavy metal pioneer. Their pounding thrash metal led to an international cult following and sales of more than 125 million albums worldwide. In addition to Hetfield and Ulrich, bassist Rob Trujillo and guitarist Kirk Hammett are current members, and prior members have included Cliff Burton and Jason Newsted, among others. Top hits include "Fade to Black" (1984), "Master of Puppets" (1986), and "One" (1988).

Onstage Metallica is wild and rambunctious, and behind the scenes they are arguably even more so, with alcohol often having compounded the band's antics in its heyday. Hetfield was especially notorious for his destructive behavior. Today, however, he is sober and the other members are taking it easier too. In interviews, Ulrich has spoken about how champagne is often his drink of choice today. But what Trujillo has described as his favorite for many years seems more representative of the band's traditional go-to: whiskey. Trujillo has shared that in the 1990s, he moved from whiskey and Coke to whiskey and ginger ale "for health reasons." His whiskey of choice was Crown Royal, which he turned to after giving up Jack Daniel's following years of overconsumption (he gave up Jägermeister for the same reason).[178]

To channel the thrash pioneers in their heyday, mix up Trujillo's favorite drink, turn the boom box up to 11, and party hard.

1 ½ ounces
Crown Royal whiskey

4 ounces ginger ale
Lime wedge

Fill a highball glass with ice and pour in the whiskey. Add ginger ale, squeeze the lime wedge juice into the glass, then drop the lime wedge in. Stir, enjoy, and thrash responsibly.

Guns N' Roses'
VODKA CRANBERRY

SERVES 1

"I'm not God but if I were God, three-quarters of you would be girls, and the rest would be pizza and beer." —Axl Rose

Hard rock band Guns N' Roses formed in 1985 and has been the band of music legends including singer Axl Rose, guitarists Slash and Izzy Stradlin, bassist Duff McKagan, keyboardist Dizzy Reed, drummer Steven Adler, and other icons. In total, the band has sold more than 100 million albums. Their top songs include such rock staples as "Welcome to the Jungle" (1987), "Sweet Child o' Mine" (1988), and "November Rain" (1992).

But the personalities who have produced such gargantuan success are also notorious for their massive consumption of alcohol and drugs, as well as for the accompanying bickering, brawls, infighting, and general destruction that went along with it. From a backstage rider, we know band members were partial to Jack Daniel's whiskey and Stoli vodka, and these preferences have also been documented by journalists who've spent time with the band.[179] In one memorable *Rolling Stone* article, a reporter who spent time with the band during its early days documented how outbursts of "mood swings" by Stradlin and Rose led to the destruction of a bottle of McKagan's vodka. In another article in more recent years, an engineer for the band commented on how McKagan always had a cup of vodka and juice with him: "the guy always had a red plastic cup filled with some liquid. Some kind of liquid . . . . I'm sure it was vodka and juice, that was his big drink at the time. He would drink vodka and then to help save his kidneys, he would drink cranberry juice."[180]

As the backstage rider also required multiple bottles of cranberry juice, we can assume the engineer's claim is legit. And although Slash is known to be a Jack Daniel's drinker, he once had an endorsement deal with the controversial company Black Death Vodka—a company that for a while sold its spirits in coffin-shaped packaging and for many years had its spirits banned in the US, and that Slash stated in interviews was a great vodka and the only kind he drank.[181] Since it was the preferred spirit for the music elite, we recommend using it here as well.

1 ounce Black Death vodka
4 ½ ounces cranberry juice
Lime wedge for garnishing

Fill a highball glass halfway with ice. Pour in vodka and cranberry juice and stir well. Garnish with the lime wedge. Sip slowly as you welcome yourself to the jungle.

1986

Lady Gaga's
JAMESON MULE

☕ ⚡ **SERVES 1**

One of today's best-selling musicians, Lady Gaga pairs her extraordinary vocal range with brilliant lyrics and piano playing to enchant fans worldwide. The New York native began playing piano at just four years old and began performing professionally in 2005. She would move to LA and release her debut album in 2008, and it would chart in the top five in the US and the peak position in many other countries. From there, her superstardom was sealed. Today Gaga has won twelve Grammys, received a Golden Globe for the film *A Star Is Born*, sold millions of albums, and is known for her eccentric style, which embraces daring cuts, sky-high heels, interesting patterns, unusual fabrics, and frequently over-the-top costumes—who can forget her meat dress, for example—in addition to many elegant designs. Among Gaga's greatest song hits are "Just Dance" (2008), "Bad Romance" (2009), and "Born This Way" (2011).

While Lady Gaga is known to be health conscious, she has also been seen relaxing with a drink on occasion. A backstage rider notes a particular preference for Kendall-Jackson or Robert Mondavi white wine, but her favorite inebriant is widely believed to be Jameson whiskey.[182] According to one outlet, she even performed at the Jameson distillery in Ireland, where she referred to the drink as her "longtime boyfriend, who was always there for me when I needed him" and dedicated a song to Jameson. Later the distillery gifted her with a five-hundred-dollar bottle of Jameson's Rarest Vintage Reserve.[183] She has even credited Jameson with being the inspiration for "Born This Way," noting on Twitter that the song was inspired by "bottles of Jameson" and "a foolish imagination."[184]

While Gaga is believed to drink Jameson without a chaser and that is certainly one way to channel her, we think she'd also approve of this Jameson mule, which brings a little ginger to the drink—a taste we know appeals to her, as ginger tea is a favorite of hers.

| 3 ounces ginger beer | ¼ ounce lime juice, freshly squeezed | Lime wedge for garnishing |
| 1 ½ ounces Jameson whiskey | ¼ ounce ginger syrup | |

Combine all ingredients except garnish in an ice-filled cocktail shaker. Shake and strain into a copper Moscow mule mug. Garnish with the lime wedge. Sip while unleashing your inner superstar and being grateful you were born this way.

PHOTO CREDITS

Pages 14 and 17: Buddy Holly publicity photos, circa 1957.

Page 18: Jimi Hendrix Experience publicity photo, 1968. Page 21: Jimi Hendrix photographed in 1970 by Detlef Hansen.

Pages 22 and 25: Janis Joplin publicity photos, 1969.

Page 26: Jim Morrison publicity photo, 1969.

Pages 28 and 31: Sister Rosetta Tharpe publicity photos, 1938.

Page 32: Elvis Presley photographed by Ollie Atkins in 1970. Page 35: *Jailhouse Rock* publicity image featuring Elvis Presley, 1957.

Page 36: John Lennon photographed by Eric Koch for ANeFo, 1969. Page 39: John Lennon in 1971, published by the University of Michigan.

Page 40: Bob Marley during an interview. Page 43: Bob Marley photographed by Patrick Lüthy, 1980.

Page 44: Freddie Mercury photographed at a press conference, 1985. Page 47: Photo of Freddie Mercury in 1977, courtesy of Carl Lender.

Pages 48 and 51: Frank Zappa in publicity photo from 1971 and 1973.

Pages 52 and 55: Photos of Jerry Garcia performing, courtesy of Carl Lender.

Page 56: Photo of Joey Ramone in 1980, courtesy of Dawkeye. Page 59: Photo of Johnny Ramone in 1990, courtesy of Masao Nakagami.

Page 60: Joe Strummer photographed in 2002 by Wwwhatsup for Punkcast. Page 63: Photo of Joe Strummer in 1980, courtesy of John Coffey.

Page 64: Johnny Cash publicity photo for CBS, 1977.

Page 66: Photo of Michael Jackson in 1993, courtesy of Constru-centro.

Page 68: Simon and Garfunkel publicity photo, 1968.

Page 70: Photo of Amy Winehouse in 2007, courtesy of Rama.

Page 72: Whitney Houston publicity photo, 1991.

Page 74: Photo of Lemmy Kilmister in 2006, courtesy of Alejandro Páez. Page 77: Photo of Lemmy Kilmister in 2011, courtesy of Rama.

Page 78: David Bowie publicity photo, 1974. Page 81: Photo of David Bowie in 1984 by Greg Gorman, courtesy of Ron Frazier.

Page 82: Photo of Prince in 2009, courtesy of Nicolas Genin.

Page 84: Chuck Berry publicity photo, circa 1958. Page 87: Chuck Berry photographed in 2008 by Pablo Vaz.

Page 88: Fats Domino photographed in 1962 by Hugo van Gelderen for ANeFo. Page 91: Fats Domino photographed in 1981 by Rob Croes for ANeFo.

Pages 92 and 95: Aretha Franklin publicity photos in 1967 and for Billboard in 1968.

Page 96: Photo of Little Richard in 2007, courtesy of Anna Bleker.

Page 98: Jerry Lee Lewis, circa 1956, photographed by Maurice Seymour.

Pages 100 and 103: Grace Slick publicity photos, 1976 and 1967.

Page 104: Tina Turner publicity photo, 1970. Page 107: Ike and Tina Turner photographed in 1971 by Rob Mieremet for ANeFo.

Page 108: Photo of Bob Dylan in 1966, courtesy of Svenska Dagbladet and IMS Vintage Photos.

Page 110: Photo of Neil Diamond in 2007, courtesy of Irisgerh.

Page 112: Photo of Carole King in 2002, courtesy of John Mathew Smith and www.celebrity-photos.com.

Page 114: Photo of Paul McCartney in 1976, courtesy of Jim Summaria. Page 116: Paul McCartney photographed in 2010 by Oli Gill.

Page 118: Joni Mitchell photographed in 1974 by Paul C. Babin.

Page 120: Keith Richards photographed in 1965 by Olavi Kaskisuo for Lehtikuva.

Pages 122 and 125: Photos of Mick Jagger in 1973, courtesy of Jens-Kristian Søgaard, and in 1965, courtesy of V. K. Hietanen.

Page 126: Roger Waters photographed in 2007 by Daigo Oliva.

Page 128: Diana Ross publicity photo, 1976. Page 131: Diana Ross photographed in 1981 by Hans van Dijk for ANeFo.

Page 132: Photo of Jimmy Page in 1977, courtesy of Jim Summaria.

Pages 134 and 137: Carly Simon publicity photos, 1972 and 1978.

Page 138: Debbie Harry in a publicity photo, 1977.

Pages 140 and 143: Photos of Eric Clapton in 1978, courtesy of Chris Hakkens, and in 1975, courtesy of Matt Gibbons.

Page 144: John Fogerty in a publicity photo, 1971.

Pages 146 and 149: Pete Townshend photographed in 1972 by Heinrich Klaffs.

Page 150: Ritchie Blackmore publicity photo, 1984. Page 153: Photo of Ritchie Blackmore in 2012, courtesy of Nsoveiko.

Page 154: Rod Stewart in a publicity photo for *Every Picture Tells A History*, 1971. Page 157: Rod Stewart photographed in 1972 by Allan Warren.

Page 158: Photo of Cher in 2019, courtesy of Ralph_PH.

Pages 160 and 163: Jimmy Buffett photographed in 1977 by the staff of Taps and in 2010 by MCCS Spike Call.

Pages 164 and 167: Photos of Linda Ronstadt in 1981, courtesy of Circacies, and in 1978, courtesy of Carl Lender.

Page 168: Photo of Patti Smith in 1978, courtesy of UCLA Library Special Collections.

Page 170: Don Henley photographed in 2019 by Derek Russell.

Page 172: Elton John photographed in 2019 by Georges Biard.

Page 174: Ian Anderson publicity photo for NBC, 1977. Page 177: Ian Anderson photographed in 1970 by Leo Luoti for Helsingin Sanomat.

Pages 178 and 181: Alice Cooper publicity photos, 1977 and 1972.

Pages 182 and 185: Photos of Donald Fagen in 2007, courtesy of Kotivalo, and in 2017, courtesy of Raph_PH.

Pages 186 and 189: Photos of Ozzy Osbourne in 2002, courtesy of John Mathew Smith and www.celebrity-photos.com, and in 2010, courtesy of Kevin Burkett.

Pages 190 and 193: Photos of Steven Tyler in 2007, courtesy of Daigo Oliva, and in 2018, courtesy of Joan017.

Pages 194 and 197: Photos of Stevie Nicks in 1980, courtesy of Ueli Frey, and in 2017, courtesy of Ralph Arvesen.

Pages 198 and 201: Photos of Billy Gibbons in 2011, courtesy of Tilly Antoine, and in 2015, courtesy of Alberto Cabello.

Page 202: Photo of Billy Joel in 2009, courtesy of David Shankbone.

Pages 204 and 207: Photos of Bruce Springsteen in 2012, courtesy of Takahiro Kyono and Bill Ebbesen.

Page 208: Photo of Gene Simmons in 2008, courtesy of Fredrik Ek.

Pages 210 and 213: Photos of Ann Wilson in 1998, courtesy of John Mathew Smith and www.celebrityphotos.com, and in 2013 courtesy of John Lill.

NOTES

1   Robert Draper, "The Real Buddy Holly," *Texas Monthly*, January 21, 2013.

2   Kevin Romig, "Not Fade Away," *Journal of Texas Music History,* vol. 11, 2011.

3   Leon Hendrix and Adam D. Mitchell, *Jimi Hendrix: A Brother's Story* (New York: Thomas Dunne Books, 2012), 136.

4   James Riordan and Jerry Prochnicky, *Break On Through: The Life and Death of Jim Morrison* (New York: William Morrow, 1991), 229.

5   "Southern Nectar," Tipsy Bartender, https://tipsybartender.com/recipe/ southern-nectar.

6   Dylan Jones, *Mr. Mojo: A Biography of Jim Morrison* (New York: Bloomsbury, 2015), 67.

7   Gale Wald, *Shout, Sister, Shout!* (New York: Beacon Press, 2007), 58.

8   Ibid.

9   Ibid., 199.

10 James Brinsford, "Elvis Presley 'Ate Same Meal for Six Months' and Banned Fish from Graceland," *Daily Mirror*, February 16, 2021.

11 Obituary of Mary Jenkins Langston, *New York Times*, June 5, 2000.

12 "Elvis Sandwich Shot," Tipsy Bartender, https://tipsybartender.com/recipe/ elvis-sandwich-shot.

13 "Why John Lennon and Harry Nilsson Got Tossed from the Troubadour," Ultimate Classic Rock, March 12, 2015, https://ultimateclassicrock.com/ john-lennon-harry-nilsson-troubadour.

14 *The Old Grey Whistle Test*, season 4, episode 28, directed by Tom Corcoran, aired April 18, 1975 on BBC2.

15 Marlon James, "Why Bob Marley Is an Underrated Style God," *GQ*, May 17, 2016.

16 Interview with Dylan Taite, "Come A Long Way," *Good Morning* (New Zealand), April 16, 1979.

17 Timothy White, *Catch a Fire: The Life of Bob Marley* (New York: Houghton Mifflin Harcourt, 1983), 258.

18 "Blog 90," freddiemercury.com, April 12, 2018, http://www.freddiemercury.com/en/ ask-phoebe/blog-90.

19 "100 Greatest Singers of All Time," *Rolling Stone*, December 3, 2010, https://www.rollingstone.com/music/ music-lists/100-greatest-singers-of-all-time-147019.

20 Erica Banas, "Supply Chain Issues May Affect Wine Production for Unexpected Reason, WMMR, October 19, 2021, https://wmmr.com/2021/10/19/supply -chain-issues-may-affect-wine-production -for-a-unexpected-reason.

21 Frank Zappa, *The Real Frank Zappa Book* (New York: Simon & Schuster, 1989), 61.

22 Dorri Olds, "Bob Zappa on Frank, Smokes and Addiction," The Fix, July 8, 2015.

23 Zappa, *The Real Frank Zappa Book*, 254.

24 "About Jerry Garcia," Dead Net, https://www.dead.net/band/jerry-garcia.

25 Grateful Dead Band Contract Rider, Jerry Garcia Official Twitter, January 4, 2022.

26 The Clash, Rock and Roll Hall of Fame website, 2003, https://www.rockhall.com/inductees/clash.

27 "The Clash's Joe Strummer Once Ran the Paris Marathon After Drinking 10 Pints of Beer," Far Out Magazine, August 21, 2020, https://faroutmagazine.co.uk/the-clash-joe-strummer-paris-marathon-beers.

28 John Sunyer, "On the Trail of Cider House Jewels," *Financial Times*, June 7, 2013.

29 Harry Sword, "West Country Cider Is a Relic from Another Century," *Vice*, November 22, 2014.

30 Johnny Cash, *Cash: The Autobiography* (San Francisco: HarperCollins, 1997), 148.

31 Fay Strang, "Michael Jackson 'Drank Six Bottles of Wine a Day in Weeks Leading to Death' Claims Friend and Godfather to His Children, Mark Lester," *Daily Mail*, April 29, 2013.

32 Tatiana Morales, "Jacko's Wine Only In Soda Cans?," CBS News, March 10, 2004.

33 "Jackson Routinely Drank Wine Out of Soda Can," TODAY.com, January 30, 2004, https://www.today.com/popculture/jackson-routinely-drank-wine-out-soda-can-wbna4109993.

34 Jane Wells, "Michael Jackson and the Neverland Wine?" CNBC, August 3, 2010.

35 "Whitney Houston's Come-Through Moment," Oprah.com, September 15, 2009, https://www.oprah.com/entertainment/the-whitney-houston-interview-continues.

36 Ian Halperin, *Whitney & Bobbi Kristina* (New York: Simon & Schuster, 2015), 255.

37 Chris Wilson, "7 Heavy Facts that Prove Motörhead's Lemmy Kilmister Was a Rock God," *Maxim*, December 29, 2015.

38 "Motörhead's Lemmy: 'I Do Still Drink A Lot. About a Bottle of Jack Daniel's A Day,'" Blabbermouth, September 28, 2009, https://www.blabbermouth.net/news/mot-rhead-s-lemmy-i-do-still-drink-a-lot-about-a-bottle-of-jack-daniel-s-a-day.

39 Michael Hann, "Lemmy: 'Apparently I am Still Indestructible,'" *The Guardian*, August 13, 2015.

40 "Tony Iommi: 'Lemmy Really Did Drink a Bottle of Whiskey a Day,'" hollywood.com, December 31, 2015, https://www.hollywood.com/general/tony-iommi-lemmy-really-did-drink-a-bottle-of-whiskey-a-day-60510873.

41 Cheryl Charming, *Miss Charming's Guide for Hip Bartenders and Wayout Wannabes* (New York: Sourcebooks, 2006), 139.

42 Ross McDonagh, "Prince Drank 'A Little Red Wine' and Never Beer...While He Thought Scotch Was 'Disgusting,' Fellow Church Member Reveals," *Daily Mail*, April 26, 2016.

43 Mikal Gilmore, "Chuck Berry, Farewell to the Father of Rock," *Rolling Stone*, April 7, 2017.

44 Chuck Berry, *Chuck Berry: The Autobiography* (New York: Fireside, 1988), 306.

45 Ibid., 305.

46   Chris Jordan, "Remembering Fats Domino," app.com, October 26, 2017, https://www.app.com/story/entertainment/music/2017/10/26/remembering-fats-domino-when-jersey-shore-visited-legend-new-orleans/801837001/.

47   Doug MacCash, "Fats Domino: Recalling the Diamonds, Red Beans, and Rock 'n' Roll," NOLA.com, October 26, 2017.

48   Aretha Franklin, Backstage Rider, The Smoking Gun, http://www.thesmokinggun.com/backstage/hall-fame/aretha-franklin.

49   Parke Puterbaugh, "Little Richard: 'I Am the Architect of Rock & Roll,'" *Rolling Stone*, April 19, 1990.

50   Rick Bragg, *Jerry Lee Lewis: His Own Story* (New York: HarperCollins, 2014), 387.

51   Ibid., 458.

52   Grace Slick, *Somebody to Love?* (New York: Hachette Book Group, 1998), 24–25.

53   "Tina Turner's Tips for Staying Sexy at 70 As She Embarks On Another World Tour," *Daily Mirror*, July 15, 2016.

54   Tina Turner, Backstage Rider, The Smoking Gun, http://www.thesmokinggun.com/file/tina-turner-rider.

55   Bob Dylan, Heaven's Door website, https://www.heavensdoor.com/straight-bourbon-whiskey.

56   Kirk Miller, "How Involved is Bob Dylan with His Whiskey Brand?," InsideHook, May 25, 2021, https://www.insidehook.com/article/booze/bob-dylan-heavens-door-whiskey-involvement.

57   Neil Diamond, "Ask Me Anything," Reddit, October 9, 2014, https://www.reddit.com/r/IAmA/comments/2jg30w/singersongwriter_neil_diamond_here_ama/.

58   Hadley Tomicki, "This Is Paul McCartney's Margarita Recipe," UrbanDaddy, February 22, 2021, https://www.urbandaddy.com/articles/43461/this-is-paul-mccartneys-margarita-recipe.

59   "Mary McCartney Shares Her Dad Paul's Favorite Margarita Recipe," Katie Couric Media, December 3, 2021, https://katiecouric.com/health/food-and-drink/mary-paul-mccartney-margarita-recipe.

60   Nick Gostin, "Mary McCartney Says Her Dad Paul Makes A Mean Margarita," *Page Six*, November 23, 2021.

61   Will Hermes, "Joni Mitchell Album Guide," *Rolling Stone*, November 7, 2019.

62   Richard Harrington, "Whatever the Promoter Will Bear," *Washington Post*, August 31, 1980.

63   Keith Richards, "Keith Richards on Mixing Vodka with Sunkist," 2003, https://www.youtube.com/watch?v=pOFgjdZmRes.

64   Patrick Doyle, "Keith Richards on Getting Busted, Zeppelin and Stones' Future," *Rolling Stone*, October 8, 2015.

65   Stephen Schiff, "Mick's Moves," *Vanity Fair*, February 1992.

66   Ibid.

67   Mary Orlin, "Cocktail Trivia: Tequila Sunrise and the Rolling Stones," Mercury News, January 20, 2016, https://www.mercurynews.com/2016/01/20/cocktail-trivia-tequila-sunrise-and-the-rolling-stones.

68   "Roger Waters Opens Up About Drug Use in Shocking Interview with Howard Stern," Society of Rock, October 25, 2019, https://societyofrock.com/roger-waters-opens-up-about-drug-use-in-shocking-interview-with-howard-stern.

69   O'Connell Driscoll, "Diana Ross: An Encounter in Three Scenes," *Rolling Stone*, August 11, 1977.

70   Ben Fong-Torres, "The Summer and Fall of Diana Ross," *Rolling Stone*, August 11, 1977.

71   J. Randy Taraborrelli, *Diana Ross: A Biography* (New York: Kensington Books, 2007), 390.

72   Cole Moreton, "'They Are Able to Consume Far More Alcohol Than I Ever Did': Led Zeppelin's Jimmy Page On the Youth of Today," *Daily Mail*, December 6, 2014.

73   Carly Simon, *Boys in the Trees* (New York: Macmillan, 2015), 127.

74   David Walters, "Blondie's Debbie Harry Just Wants a Big Bowl of Buttercream," *Bon Appétit*, April 7, 2017.

75   Ibid.

76   Eric Clapton, *Clapton: The Autobiography* (New York: Random House, 2007), 217.

77   "Eric Clapton Admits to Making Alcoholic Strange Brew," Celebretainment.com, January 9, 2018, https://www.celebretainment.com/celebrities/eric-clapton-admits-to-making-alcoholic-strange-brew/article_0a87c094-e736-5fd5-90f0-d8104db4db21.html.

78   John Fogerty, *Fortunate Son* (New York: Little, Brown, 2015), 401.

79   David Cheal, "Pete Townshend and Roger Daltrey on Drugs, Drummers and Fish," *Financial Times*, March 19, 2019.

80   Pete Townshend, *Pete Townshend: Who I Am* (London: HarperCollins, 2012), 223.

81   Mara Siegler, "Pete Townshend: Being a Rock Star Fuels Addiction," Page Six, May 29, 2015, https://pagesix.com/2015/05/29/pete-townshend-being-a-rock-star-fuels-addiction.

82   Cameron Crowe, "Ritchie Blackmore: Shallow Purple," *Rolling Stone*, April 10, 1975.

83   Peter Makowski, "Rainbow Rising: How Ritchie Blackmore Aimed for the Stars," *Louder Sound*, April 14, 2014.

84   Dominic Roskrow, "Scotch on the Rocks," *Whisky Magazine*, https://whiskymag.com/story?Scotch-on-the-rocks.

85   Marielle Anas, "Life Advice from Rod Stewart," *Men's Journal*, February 1, 2016.

86   Rod Stewart, *Rod: The Autobiography* (London: Century, 2012), 130.

87   Lydia Spencer-Elliott, "Cher, 75, Struggles in Her High Heels as She Steps Out for Cocktails," *Daily Mail*, July 17, 2021.

88   Taffy Brodesser-Akner, "Jimmy Buffett Does Not Live the Jimmy Buffett Lifestyle," *New York Times*, February 11, 2018.

89   Jimmy Buffett, "This is Jimmy Buffett's Legendary Margarita Recipe," *InStyle*, June 13, 2018.

90   Linda Ronstadt, *Simple Dreams: A Musical Memoir* (New York: Simon & Schuster, 2013), 103.

91   Ben Fong-Torres, "Heartbreak on Wheels," *Rolling Stone*, March 27, 1975.

92   Christopher Bollen, "Patti Smith and Robert Mapplethorpe," *Interview Magazine*, January 12, 2010.

93   Anwen Crawford, "The Theology of Patti Smith," *New Yorker*, October 6, 2015.

94   Paul Lester, "Don Henley: 'There's No Partying, No Alcohol, It's Like a Morgue Backstage,'" *The Guardian*, October 1, 2015.

95   Tom Bryant, "Music Legend Don Henley On His New Healthy Life On the Road After Rock and Roll Excesses of The Eagles," *Daily Mirror*, September 29, 2015.

96   Marc Eliot, *To the Limit: The Untold Story of the Eagles* (New York: Little, Brown, 1998), 206.

97   Sarah Deen, "Elton John 'Drank a Bottle of Whisky a Day' When Battle with Alcoholism Was At Its Worst," *Metro*, November 19, 2019.

98   Johnnie Walker website, https://www.johnniewalker.com/en/whisky-cocktails/highball-cocktails/johnnie-lemon-highball/.

99   Michael Friedman, "Ian Anderson's Progressive Path," *Psychology Today*, June 20, 2016, https://www.psychologytoday.com/us/blog/brick-brick/201606/ian-anderson-s-progressive-path.

100   Paul Elliot, "Ian Anderson Interview: The Beginning, Middle and End of Jethro Tull," Louder Sound, April 2, 2020, https://www.loudersound.com/features/ian-anderson-interview-the-beginning-middle-and-end-of-jethro-tull.

101   Steve Morse, "Ian Anderson On 50 Years of Jethro Tull, Tinny Garden Acoustics, and Never Being Too Old to Rock and Roll," *Boston Globe*, September 5, 2019.

102   "Alice Cooper's Alcohol Cookbook: The Band's Favorite Drink Recipes As Told To Creem," *Creem*, June 1973.

103   Derek Robertson, "Are You Relivin' the Years?: How Steely Dan Became a Cult Favorite for Millennials," *The Ringer*, July 21, 2021, https://www.theringer.com/music/2021/7/21/22586128/steely-dan-popular-cult-favorite-millennials.

104   Ozzy Osbourne, *I Am Ozzy* (New York: Hachette, 2011), 415–416.

105   Bill Sullivan, "Gene's Addiction, or Why Ozzy Osbourne Is Still Alive," *Discover Magazine*, October 10, 2019.

106   "Ozzy Osbourne: 'Hunting the Salami' and Hangover Cures," *The Times*, December 5, 2010.

107   Annie Karni, "'Idol's' Tyler Tries Walking Straight & Aero," *New York Post*, January 23, 2011.

108   Stephen Tyler, *Does the Noise in My Head Bother You?* (New York: HarperCollins, 2011), 160.

109   Craig McLean, "Stevie Nicks: The Men, the Music, the Menopause," *The Guardian*, March 25, 2011.

110   Stevie Nicks, Backstage Rider, The Smoking Gun, www.thesmokinggun.com/backstage/divas/stevie-nicks-0.

111   Nick Paumgarten, "Gibbons," *New Yorker*, November 27, 2005.

112   ZZ Top, Backstage Rider, The Smoking Gun, http://www.thesmokinggun.com/backstage/hall-fame/zz-top.

113   Corey Irwin, "How ZZ Top Got Past Their Manager's Two-Drink Limit," Ultimate Classic Rock, February 25, 2020, https://ultimateclassicrock.com/zz-top-manager-drink-limit/.

114   Pura Vida Tequila website, https://www.puravidatequila.com.

115   Billy Gibbons, "Billy Gibbons Signature Pura Vida Tequila Cocktail – The Gibbons," May 5, 2015, https://www.youtube.com/watch?v=yOM_ljR9HP8.

116   Bruce Springsteen, *Born to Run* (New York: Simon & Schuster, 2016), 291.

117   Melek Nur Pervan, "The Real Reason Why Gene Simmons Hasn't Drink Alcohol In His Entire Life," Rock Celebrities, June 4, 2021, https://rockcelebrities.net/the-real-reason-why-gene-simmons-hasnt-drink-alcohol-in-his-entire-life.

118   Gene Simmons, Twitter post, January 1, 2020, http://twitter.com/genesimmons.

119   Ann Wilson and Nancy Wilson, *Kicking & Dreaming* (New York: It Books, 2012), 253.

120   Heart, Backstage Rider, The Smoking Gun, 2002, http://www.thesmokinggun.com/file/heart-backstage-rider.

121   Suzi Quatro, *Unzipped* (London: Hodder & Stoughton, 2007), 154.

122 Anthi Charalambous, "'Inside I Feel 30ish - I'm Childish and Optimistic': Under the Microscope with Suzi Quatro," *Daily Mail*, October 25, 2011.

123 Chrissie Hynde, *Reckless: My Life as a Pretender* (New York: Knopf, 2015), 92.

124 The Pretenders, Backstage Rider, The Smoking Gun, http://www.thesmokinggun.com/backstage/hall-fame/pretenders.

125 David Fricke, "John Cougar Mellencamp: The Comeback Kid," *Rolling Stone*, January 31, 1986.

126 John Mellencamp, Backstage Rider, The Smoking Gun, 1998, http://www.thesmokinggun.com/backstage/hall-fame/john-mellencamp.

127 Christopher Connelly, "Hey, John Cougar, What's Your Problem?," *Rolling Stone*, December 9, 1982.

128 Martin Torgoff, *American Fool: The Roots and Improbable Rise of John Cougar Mellencamp* (New York: Macmillan, 1986), 35.

129 Sting, Backstage Rider, The Smoking Gun, 2000, http://www.thesmokinggun.com/backstage/arena-rock/sting-0.

130 "Sting," Star.Wine website, https://www.star.wine/en/sting.

131 Patrick Schmitt, "Sting: I Make Good Wine As Revenge," *The Drinks Business*, April 12, 2017.

132 Elizabeth Day, "Interview: The Thing About Sting...," *The Guardian*, September 24, 2011.

133 "Strawberry Italian Soda," Mom Timeout, May 9, 2021, https://www.momontimeout.com/strawberry-italian-soda-recipe.

134 David Lee Roth, "Alcohol & Cigarettes," *The Roth Show*, April 1, 2013.

135 "Van Halen's Legendary M&M's Rider," The Smoking Gun, December 11, 2008, http://www.thesmokinggun.com/documents/crime/van-halens-legendary-mms-rider.

136 Alex Williams, "Afternoon Beers with a Former Sex Pistol," *New York Times*, September 28, 2018.

137 John Lydon, "John Lydon," *Wall Street Journal*, April 25, 2013.

138 Belinda Carlisle, *Lips Unsealed* (New York: Crown, 2010), 87.

139 *Bad Reputation,* directed by Kevin Kerslake (Magnolia Pictures, 2018).

140 Ibid.

141 David Fricke, "Joan Jett: Built to Rock," *Rolling Stone*, April 24, 2015.

142 "Madonna's Got a Pretty Demanding Tour Rider," iHeart Radio, March 3, 2016, https://www.iheartradio.net.nz/music-news/madonnas-got-a-pretty-demanding-tour-rider.

143 Madonna, Instagram Post, November 18, 2021, https://www.instagram.com/p/CWbzLbPvyWDe.

144 *Victoria Wood's Nice Cup of Tea* (BBC, 2013).

145 Shawn Amos, "Eternal Flame: 10 Questions with Susanna Hoffs," *HuffPost*, March 17, 2009.

146 Kelly McCartney, "Susanna Hoffs Talks About Hotness, Aging, and Love," Kelly McCartney blog, https://thekelword.wordpress.com/2012/09/30/susanna-hoffs-talks-about-hotness-aging-and-love.

147 U2, Backstage Rider, The Smoking Gun, 1992, http://www.thesmokinggun.com/file/u2.

148 Adam Block, "Bono Bites Back," *Mother Jones*, May 1, 1989.

149   Nicole Lampert, "Beach Boy Who Grew Up," *Daily Mail Weekend Magazine*, June 24, 2019.

150   Rebecca Nicholson, "The Breeders on Kicking Drugs, Kurt Cobain and Life After the Pixies," *The Guardian*, October 7, 2017.

151   Noah Rothbaum, "Jon Bon Jovi Is Trying to Change the Wine World," Daily Beast, March 5, 2018, https://www.thedailybeast.com/jon-bon-jovi-is-trying-to-change-the-wine-world.

152   Bon Jovi, Backstage Rider, The Smoking Gun, http://www.thesmokinggun.com/backstage/arena-rock/bon-jovi-0.

153   Alyssa Shelasky, "Courtney Love Is Hooked on Chicken Potpie and Pineapple Upside-Down Cake," *New York Magazine*, May 4, 2012.

154   Ibid.

155   "Unfiltered," *Wine Spectator*, May 17, 2006.

156   Stephanie Rafanelli, "How Mr Lenny Kravitz Keeps His Cool," Mr Porter, December 14, 2017, https://www.mrporter.com/en-us/journal/lifestyle/how-mr-lenny-kravitz-keeps-his-cool-1103218.

157   "12 Questions: Lenny Kravitz," *Lux Magazine*, Autumn 2019.

158   Jonathan Van Meter, "The Outer Limits," *Spin*, December 1997.

159   Lisa Robinson, "New Again: Janet Jackson," *Interview Magazine*, October 13, 2016.

160   "Janet Jackson Grabs Cocktails with Girlfriends," *People*, August 12, 2009.

161   *Now More Than Ever: The History of Chicago*, directed by Peter Pardini (2016; Los Angeles, CA: CNN Film, Chicago Records II, and Sonder Entertainment).

162   "On the Horn with Jimmy," *Oregon Wine Magazine*, October 1, 2016.

163   Ibid.

164   Diana Rojo-Garcia, "Bringing Joy to This World," *Mankato Free Press*, June 14, 2018.

165   Libby Copeland, "Dave Grohl Is A Back-Aching, Coffee-Guzzling, Minivan-Driving Classic Rocker," *Washington Post*, June 26, 2015.

166   Martin Kielty, "Dave Grohl Reveals Hour-Long Drinking Session Before Each Show," Ultimate Classic Rock, September 26, 2018, https://ultimateclassicrock.com/dave-grohl-drinking-before-show.

167   "Deer and Beer," Jägermeister website, https://www.jagermeister.com/en-US/drinks/beer-and-deer.

168   Leonie Cooper, "Holly-Back Girl: Gwen Stefani On How to Have the Perfect Christmas," *NME*, December 17, 2017.

169   Angus Young and Cliff Williams, "Ask Me Anything," Reddit, November 15, 2014, https://www.reddit.com/r/IAmA/comments/2mebk6/we_are_angus_young_and_cliff_williams_from_acdc.

170   Alex Pappademas, "Foolish, Foolish Throat: A Q&A with Steve Perry," *GQ*, May 29, 2008.

171   Journey, Backstage Rider, The Smoking Gun, 2001, http://www.thesmokinggun.com/backstage/cutout-bin/journey-0.

172   Alex James, *Bit of a Blur* (New York: Little, Brown, 2008), 77.

173   Jenn Harris, "Fergie Hosts Charity Cocktail Party, Likes Her Own Vodka," *Los Angeles Times*, December 7, 2012.

174   Sukriti Wahi, "Shakira's Exact Diet & Exercise Routine," *Marie Claire*, October 15, 2020.

175   Lizzy Goodman, "'I Wanted to Get In There Like a Motherf**ker': The Story of Karen O," *Elle*, May 22, 2017, https://www.elle.com/culture/music/a45458/karen-o-oral-history.

176   Ibid.

177 "Pink's Preferred Name for a Baby Boy: Jameson," *People*, November 29, 2010.

178 Derek Brown, "Drinking With Metallica's Rob Trujillo," Punch, May 30, 2014, https://punchdrink.com/articles/drinking-with-metallicas-rob-trujillo.

179 Guns N' Roses, Backstage Rider, The Smoking Gun, http://www.thesmokinggun.com/backstage/hall-fame/guns-n-roses.

180 "Engineer Talks How Axl Rose Behaved While Making GN'R's 'Appetite,' Recalls Duff McKagan's Shocking Drinking Habits," Ultimate Guitar, May 25, 2021, https://www.ultimate-guitar.com/news/general_music_news/engineer_talks_how_axl_rose_behaved_while_making_gnrs_appetite_recalls_duff_mckagans_shocking_drinking_habits.html.

181 "Guns N' Roses: True Story Behind Slash & Black Death Vodka!" GNR Central, October 1, 2018, https://gnrcentral.com/2018/10/01/guns-n-roses-true-story-behind-slash-black-death-vodka.

182 Lady Gaga, Backstage Rider, The Smoking Gun, 2010, http://www.thesmokinggun.com/backstage/divas/lady-gaga-10.

183 Amy Andrews, "Lady Gaga Shows Up at Jameson Brewery and Calls the Whiskey Her "Longtime Boyfriend," Irish Central, October 29, 2010, https://www.irishcentral.com/opinion/amyandrews/lady-gaga-shows-up-at-jameson-brewery-and-calls-the-whiskey-her-longtime-boyfriend-106284153-238050571

184 Lady Gaga, Twitter Post, May 26, 2011, https://twitter.com/ladygaga/status/73958227972325376.